Praise for The *Christian Zo...*

Zombies are everywhere these days. Th...
The Walking Dead is one of the most p...
is starring in a major new motion pictur, *world War Z*. There's even
zombie music out there by artists such as Aaron Stoquert.

What you won't find are Christian zombie books. Sure, there are
plenty of horror writers who are Christians, myself included. But few,
if any, have ever combined their faith with their stories, at least not
overtly. Like oil and water, the two just don't seem to mix.

So, how did Jeff Kinley manage it? And more important, why?

Let's be clear: this volume is *unique*. A word often used but in this
case thoroughly deserved. Jeff has found a way to communicate God's
grace to a new audience. It's culturally relevant, deeply perceptive, and
really inspires us to discover the truth for ourselves.

In this volume, you will find a gripping, face-paced zombie survival story as good as any you'll read in a mainstream horror novel or
see in the latest Romero film. But you'll also find a parallel commentary providing a startlingly honest insight and unique perspective on
our struggle with sin.

As he does week in, week out, Jeff is reaching out to us to deliver
God's Word in a style and language that we can all understand.
Particularly those of us fascinated by zombies . . .

At the same time, he really leaves you wondering—*Who really is
the zombie here?* And when I really think about it—why do I keep struggling with the same sins and turning away from God? Time after time?

What more could you want? Here's a pastor who will help you survive the zombies and open your eyes to the startling truth that only by
truly trusting in Christ as our Saviour can we all survive the zombies.

I certainly want Jeff on my team when the undead shamble into
town. And the Lord—well, we only have to ask and He'll always be
with us.

—**Sean T. Page**, author of *War Against the Walking Dead* and *The Official
Zombie Handbook*

THE CHRISTIAN ZOMBIE KILLER'S HANDBOOK

SLAYING THE LIVING DEAD WITHIN

BY JEFF KINLEY

THOMAS NELSON
Since 1798

NASHVILLE DALLAS MEXICO CITY RIO DE JANEIRO

Published in Nashville, Tennessee, by Thomas Nelson. Thomas Nelson is a registered trademark of Thomas Nelson, Inc.

Thomas Nelson, Inc., titles may be purchased in bulk for educational, business, fund-raising, or sales promotional use. For information, please e-mail SpecialMarkets@ThomasNelson.com.

Unless otherwise indicated, Scripture quotations are taken from the Holy Bible, New International Version®. NIV® © 1973, 1978, 1984, 2010 by Biblica, Inc.™ Used by permission of Zondervan. All rights reserved worldwide. www.zondervan.com

Scripture quotations marked ESV are taken from the ENGLISH STANDARD VERSION. © 2001 by Crossway Bibles, a division of Good News Publishers.

Scripture quotations marked KJV are from the King James Version.

Scripture quotations marked MSG are taken from *The Message* by Eugene H. Peterson. © 1993, 1994, 1995, 1996, 2000. Used by permission of NavPress Publishing Group. All rights reserved.

Scripture quotations marked NASB are taken from the NEW AMERICAN STANDARD BIBLE®. © The Lockman Foundation 1960, 1962, 1963, 1968, 1971, 1972, 1973, 1975, 1977. Used by permission.

Scripture quotations marked NLT are taken from the *Holy Bible*, New Living Translation. © 1996. Used by permission of Tyndale House Publishers, Inc., Wheaton, Illinois 60189. All rights reserved.

Author's note: The episodes in this book are fictional, and as such, some of the statistics, events, people, places, and works in them are imaginary.

Library of Congress Cataloging-in-Publication Data

Kinley, Jeff.
  The Christian zombie killers handbook : slaying the living dead within / by Jeff Kinley.
    p. cm.
  Includes bibliographical references.
  ISBN 978-1-59555-438-3 (alk. paper)
    1. Sin—Christianity—Miscellanea. 2. Salvation—Christianity—Miscellanea. 3. Zombies—Miscellanea. I. Title.
  BT715.K57 2011
  241'.3—dc22   2011013380

Printed in the United States of America

11 12 13 14 15 QG 6 5 4 3 2 1

TO STUART

CONTENTS

Contents

INTRODUCTION

Zombies are real. And they are among us.

We have a problem here. I do, and you do too. It's a dilemma found deep inside the darkest part of your heart. In a damp dungeon of the soul. In a corner of the human psyche where a ravenous beast dwells. This monster is sinister, deceptive, wicked, and vile . . . beyond belief. It's the part of you that loves to do what is wrong. It takes great pleasure in seeing life revolve around its huge ego. It thrives on satisfying its every desire. It is the ultimate narcissist. The poster child for self-absorption, it walks a thin line between shallow insecurity and egotistical conceit.

But, the reality remains—there is a devil inside you. Lurking, lusting, longing to take control.

Introduction

Despite what you might want, you can't just go kill it. There is no magic ministry formula, no special Christian recipes for disposing of it. You can't simply delete it from your life or drag it out to the trash for someone to haul away. You can't send Special Forces in after it. It is well hidden. Embedded. Stealthily concealed lest you catch it out in the open. It stalks you from within, ready in the tick of a heart-beat to pounce on you and devour you.

Deny it if you dare. Try and ignore it if you can. But this thing inside you is as real as the page you are looking at. It exists for one reason—to haunt you. It loves to hurt you. It desires to rule over you. To master your every movement. It hates anything and everything that is pure and honorable about you.

And more than anything, it *detests* God.

This ancient evil is a monster, and when it is awakened, a door to hell itself is opened, spewing forth a barrage of malevolence and sin.

This monster is known by many names. The Flesh. The Sin Nature. The Old Man. Even The Heart. From an early age, it introduces you to a world of self-worship, a solar system in which every pursuit revolves in a ceaseless orbit around self.

This creature within you is a carnivorous being that, despite all your efforts and church-fueled formulas, will simply not die. It is your constant companion. Your Siamese twin, joined at the heart.

The monster is *you*. Or at least a big part of you.

Should you dare to find out where it lives, it will require descending to the place where it dwells. But be forewarned. You must prepare yourself for sights, sounds, and smells that will turn your stomach and repulse the senses. For as we shine the light of truth on it, its hideous appearance will gradually become evident. And the mirror's reflection may be more than you can stand.

Welcome to your own personal Planet Zombie.

LEGEND OF THE LIVING DEAD

Ben Forman couldn't breathe. Hyperventilating, he struggled to control the shallow gasps entering and exiting his body.

"Just . . . breathe . . . Don't . . . p-p-panic," he muttered to himself.

Just seconds earlier, Ben was nonchalantly reading a text message he'd just received. Strange how life can change in a few ticks of a clock. In the time it takes to read this sentence, your perspective on life can be suddenly inverted, forever altering your perception of reality. That's what happened to Ben. And he would never be the same.

That was last night.

Ben is a twenty-four-year-old graphic artist working in downtown Corazon City, a community located in the Smoky Mountains of North Carolina. Nestled in a picturesque valley, the city is virtually surrounded by scenic mountains.

Ben Forman moved back to his hometown six months ago after accepting a job at *Sk8X*, a magazine devoted to the sport of extreme skateboarding. Ben is making the transition from starving freelance artist to full-time "professional." So his future was starting to ramp up. Or so it seemed.

Ben is 5 feet, 9 inches tall, 150 pounds, with piercing blue eyes and uncombed black hair. His clothes are mostly thrift-store finds. He's not much for material possessions, climbing the corporate ladder, athletics, or even skateboards, for that matter. Even so, he dove right into his new job, immersing himself into the subculture of extreme skateboarding, learning along the way. And when he isn't working on a project, he's usually hanging out with girlfriend Crystal.

He's a working man, and though he isn't yet making much money by industry standards, it's enough for him, for now.

Now on to what happened last night. It was Wednesday around ten thirty when Ben finally left Sk8X. The company is located in a converted warehouse on the city's south side, near the old railroad depot. Sk8X rents out the top floor. So after staying late at work, Ben was walking toward his car while reading a text from Crystal. But just after shoving the phone back into his jeans pocket, he hit something slippery on the sidewalk, nearly doing a classic skateboard wipeout. Turning to look at what caused his misstep, Ben noticed under the streetlamp's glow a shiny puddle of red gathering at his feet. Tracking with his eyes, he traced the scarlet flow all the way to its source. And that's when he saw the body.

Or what was left of it.

It was clearly a man, though the top part of his head was missing, and the brain was gone. Skin and other body parts were randomly scattered around the motionless corpse. The man's right hand still clutched a set of car keys. A well-worn backpack lay beside him. His shirt ripped and shredded. His jeans slightly scuffed at the knees. But his skull was grossly disfigured, pressed facedown in a glistening, gory pool of still-oozing crimson.

Upon this gruesome discovery, Ben's first instinct was to yell for help, but *nothing* came out of his mouth. Not a sound. It took him several tries until his fingers stopped shaking long enough to dial 999.

• • •

Authorities investigating the grizzly crime scene estimated the man was in his early-to-mid-thirties. After gathering evidence, they speculated that he was murdered and mutilated by a minimum of five or six attackers. His brain was removed and then eaten. *Eaten!* Raw. Episodes like this seem to appear with greater regularity these days, though they don't always end up like this. Or at least it's not reported as much. Ever since the national threat level was raised to level 3, such attacks have been on the rise . . . even in places like beautiful Corazon City. You expect this kind of crime somewhere like New York, L.A., or Chicago, but this is the foothills of the Smokies. And it was the second attack downtown in as many months. This poor guy was one of the lucky ones, actually. He was still recognizable. Several past attacks have been so brutal that authorities have had to use dental records to determine the victim's identity. And when all that's left of you is bone and teeth . . . well . . . let's just say you really don't want to die like that.

As the frequency of attacks has increased nationally in the past two decades, security has stepped up on every level. Several years back, then governor Johnston earmarked more than $40 million to beef up law enforcement and hire more police officers. He also partnered with neighboring states to help launch the establishment of a permanent training facility in the nearby Chattahoochee National Forest in Georgia. With North Carolina leading the way, other states were inspired to create their own state-run special forces groups, designed specifically to hunt down and kill any confirmed flesh-eater. The strategy caught on nationwide, and ultimately in 2002 the federal government took over, forming what we now know as the "ZTF" (Zombie Task Force). This mandate from the White House came at the right time, especially in light of the steadily increasing number of murders and mutilations. It became clear that what was needed was an elite, core group of highly trained soldiers, snipers, and intelligence officers to work closely with the Centers for Disease Control to battle these monsters. The CDC was brought in to contain the symptoms associated with what is now known as the Z-38 virus and attacks related to it. If a victim didn't get his head smashed in and brains eaten, he or she could still get bitten or mauled, and thus infected. And getting infected means fever, swelling, tremors, vomiting, disorientation, dementia, insanity, and eventually, death. So far, the CDC has only been able to quarantine infected citizens, observing and treating the symptoms, and has achieved moderate success. Past studies have indicated that some patients initially showed positive signs of recovery; however, leading researchers now believe this so-called success is nothing more than false hope, dismissing it as the effects of heavy sedation. Now experts are saying the virus can go "underground," lying dormant in the body for months, even years, before randomly resurfacing and producing symptoms and behavior associated with full-fledged flesh-eaters. The victim, going about normal daily life, can in just hours undergo a transformation and violently attack and devour a family member, neighbor, coworker, in-law, or friend, for no apparent reason. In extreme cases, the infected will even engage in a bizarre form of "self-mutilation," eating his or her own flesh and brains, until death occurs. Bizarre indeed.

Despite the long history of this phenomenon, it's still hotly debated where it actually came from. Theories of the virus's origin and how it spread are too many to list here. But a simple web search will yield a huge camp of conspiracy theorists. One of these even claims our own government developed and released the virus into our drinking supply.

But most people subscribe to one of three leading theories. The first involves the notion that about six thousand years ago there was some sort of weird, spontaneous chromosomal mutation. This mutation spawned a peculiar race of humans whose DNA genetically predisposed them to an acute appetite for human flesh. There are grandiose mythological tales of human sacrifice in ancient Sumeria (present-day Iraq), where these mutant humans were treated like—even feared as—*gods*. Local tribes, afraid of being eaten, staged weekly sacrificial ceremonies. In these quasi-religious rites (so the legend goes), six human sacrifices, within six months of their twenty-first birthdays, were bound by horsehair ropes and ceremoniously led to a series of altars. There, each was given a cocktail of wine mixed with poppy plant extract to produce a chemically induced trance. Disoriented, the sacrifices' senses were dulled and their bodies numb. Then they were laid on their backs, and the high priests of this carnivorous cult took a sharpened stone and literally sawed off the top of each victim's skull while he or she was still conscious! The brains were then eaten by the "gods."

These brain-hungry mutants eventually intermarried, ultimately producing a superior race of humanlike creatures whose main diet consisted of flesh and cranial tissue. Expanding in concentric circles out of ancient Sumeria, they continued breeding and infecting humanity—from Egypt to Africa, Palestine to Rome, Rome to Europe, and eastward toward what eventually became China.

As crazy as this theory sounds, archaeological digs around the Tigris-Euphrates river system uncovered what appears to be a temple-like structure with "thrones," accompanied by a series of crude altars, each the length of a human body.

Coincidence? There are also stone reliefs in the walls of this temple, depicting scenes in which kings or rulers are eating out of the heads of slaves. While adherents of this theory claim this is solid evidence of the flesh-eaters' true beginnings, skeptics contend that this was nothing more than an ancient cult, confined to the region and with no historical significance.

Another equally peculiar hypothesis suggests that the genesis of last night's murderous rampage can be traced back millions of years to when our planet was actually a substation for a humanlike alien race. The purpose of this pilgrim settlement wasn't to colonize a new world or expand some extraterrestrial kingdom. It wasn't established as a place to escape persecution or engage in intergalactic exploration. In this scenario of origins, those loaded onto spaceships and sent to our world were the absolute undesirables of their native planet. Hardcore criminals. Death-row inmates. "Scum-of-the-earth" types (or whatever *their* world was called). Though meant as a punishment, being deposited on our pristine, green globe was a merciful sentence, all things considered. Our planet was like a welcoming bus stop where the aliens were dropped off and expected to make it on their own. Which they did without much difficulty. At first.

Then something happened. And there's speculation here. Perhaps something about Earth's atmosphere didn't mix well with their immune systems (assuming they had developed them). Could've been something they ingested. Some random chemical malfunction in their biological makeup. No one knows. But instead of working together to build a fresh life in their new world, rival gangs of these extraterrestrials revolted against each other and began slaughtering their alien brothers. But it didn't end with murder. Notwithstanding the abundance of animals and fresh meat in plentiful supply here, these criminals began devouring one another instead. *Not* as some cannibalistic symbol of tribal domination. But for *food*. For sustenance. Even for *pleasure*!

Then they reproduced, making more beings like themselves over the centuries, and, well, here we are. Sounds hard to swallow, sure. But it does remain one of the top three theories. You may be surprised at how many people subscribe to this belief. They claim that proof of more recent "visitations" is soundly documented with eyewitness accounts, geographical land markings, and even photographs (though most believe they're photoshopped). Nonetheless, this theory has never gained traction with the government and the established scientific community. Something about the "lack of sufficient credible evidence."

The last major theory of zombie origins is found in "the Old Way," of which you've surely heard. This one has significant support in virtually every culture, both ancient and modern. The tradition (whose followers are called "Believers") claims that all humanity can be traced back to two common ancestors, created thousands of years ago by a mysterious, invisible deity. This divine being had created a perfect, germ-free, ecologically balanced environment, untouched by darkness or any bad thing. This god designed his creation to be a tribe of worshippers. There was no pain, suffering, or death. No human vices or diseases. And no rotting flesh or the awful, putrid smell that accompanies it. Theirs was a perfect environment.

Not long after this, the created ones sensed there was something better for them. Something *more*. Something beyond what their creator had provided. And so, without permission, they broke away from the oppressive restrictions placed on them, creating instead their own reality, one in which no supreme being would dictate their lives or presume to know what was best for them. In an instant, they decided that their life-giver would cease to meddle in their affairs and would no longer tell them what to think, feel, or do. No longer would he impede their progress toward self-realization and self-discovery. So they summarily voted their maker off their earth-island paradise in light of a more immediate and pleasurable existence.

"But," the Believers claim, "this move brought devastating consequences to humanity."[1] And this, they say, is the origin of the virus so prevalent in today's flesh-eaters. However, if you think about it, there must have been something already inside them, predisposing them to contracting this virus. Something had to trigger it out of its incubative state, where it slowly spread to the central nervous system and finally to the brain, where it took over.

The virus then manifested itself through things humanity had never experienced before—like shame. Guilt. Sadness. Loneliness. Separation. Disappointment. Bitterness. Depression. Grief. Anger. Hate. Rage. And ultimately . . . insatiable flesh-hunger and murder. It didn't take long for earth's tiny population to begin delving into this supreme dark art form. Legend says the first human to kill another did so with a crushing rock-blow to the skull. And it went progressively downhill from there. Through procreation, each successive offspring became more genetically prone to a fleshly passion.

This inherently religio-biological explanation for mankind's beginning has yet to convince everyone of its veracity. What is known, and what seems to harmonize with this particular theory of origins, is that the propensity for zombie-ism crosses every national and international boundary, just as adherents to the Old Way claim. The flesh-eaters are in every culture on the planet. Even in remote tribes. Whatever causes this behavior appears to be no respecter of gender, race, age, nationality, or religious creed. It affects literally every kind of person. Small and great. Rich and poor alike.

An equal-opportunity curse.

It's conceivable that these origin theories could've been

formulated by observing mankind's current problem and then simply concocting a theory to accommodate it. A sort of "retroactive genesis of origins." Of course, many reject the Old Way's explanation because, again, there doesn't appear to be hard, reproducible scientific evidence for their ideas. And because it sounds way too religious, of course. In fact, some in the Old Way are ridiculed as "old-fashioned" or dismissed as "nutcases."

Bottom line: no one—religious nutcase or rational scientist—can deny the existence of this murderous, brain-eating behavior. That's something we all agree on. And if you're honest, you'd confess to entertaining the fear that at some point in your life, a fellow human will, without warning, suddenly "go zombie" on you, forcibly escorting you to a violent and painful death. And then gobble up your brain! It's not the type of thing people talk about at dinner parties or in the company break room. Not the conversation you overhear while standing in line at the grocery store or in the school lunchroom.

But you know it's what you think about when you're alone in your room at night. In those virgin moments of silence just after the bedside light goes off. *That's* when your mind is most likely to be flooded with *zombie-dread*. It's the fear of the unknown, really. The terror that lurks in the dark. Around the corner. Behind the door. Down that long hallway.

Under your bed.

It's the unspoken horror-thought of not knowing whether *you'll* be next. Of wondering if you'll be the main course at the next communal flesh-feast. And in those final seconds before falling asleep, you wonder if the eventual attack will be from someone you know—a classmate, coworker, friend, husband, or wife. That makes zombies the ultimate bogeymen.

The world really is messed up . . . beyond belief. And it's getting scarier every day.

And now you know why Ben Forman couldn't breathe.

Chapter 1

I AM LEGEND

We are each our own devil, and we make this world
our hell.

—Oscar Wilde

Evil enters like a needle and spreads like an oak tree.

—Ethiopian proverb

Something's in the Air

From the beginning of recorded history, humankind
has been plagued with a weakness for wickedness. An
irresistible, gravitational pull toward moral insanity. Perhaps
this is why every reputable religion recognizes a basic moral
code, and even in the most remote tribes there is always some
inherent understanding of basic *right* and *wrong*. This intrinsic
trend toward morality (both for and against it) was something
affirmed in Scripture more than two thousand years ago.[1]

But the real question is, *why* do humans do wicked things?
Do mankind's heinous acts stem from some inherent evil that
dwells inside us? Or could it be that we're actually not responsible for our actions, no matter how cruel or wrong they may
seem? Is there an evil presence within us? Or does "badness"
just randomly leap on us at unfortunate times, like a black cat

out of a dark alley? What influences a person to lie? Why are we infected with hate, lust, murder, and abuse? Why are we so bound up in our individual cocoons of self-absorption, seemingly unable to escape? Why are we so *bad*? And why does this decadent disease affect every person—from the great to the small? Male and female? Old and young? Civilized and barbarian? Religious and pagan? Ancient or postmodern?

Why can't Christians concentrate on God for more than a few minutes at a time without our minds jumping to another subject? Why does focusing on him seem so unnatural? At the same time we are engrossed in movies, sports, or video games for hours. We can cuddle up with sinful thoughts without interruption, and yet struggle to find an unbroken minute of pure reflection or spiritual meditation.

Why?

The truth is that you and I are both intuitively trained from within and highly skilled in the art of sin. Our default mode is *self* and *anti*-God.

We are hard-wired for wickedness. Programmed for a high-octane pursuit of soul-crimes.

We hate God.

And this makes us not want to want him. So where did all this evil come from? How was it set in motion? To gain some clarity on this issue, our journey takes us to the Book of Beginnings, better known as Genesis.

Recapping Moses' record of early humanity, many years ago the Creator made one man and one woman,[2] placing them into a perfect garden environment called Eden.[3] It was a paradise of unimaginable beauty. Nothing on our planet compares to it. Not even close. Colors were still in their original brilliance and hues. Fresh garden food was abundant and delicious. A perfect temperature saturated this garden and suited the human body, especially considering that Eden's inhabitants lived there naked.

There were no thorns. No poisonous plants. No parasites. No pesky bugs to bite them. It was an unspoiled ecosystem. The entire animal kingdom coexisted in symphonic harmony with nature. It was a glorious song. Our present world is like a faded photograph in comparison.

But creation's beauty was only a faint reflection of the melodious refrain sung by the man and woman to their God. The first humans enjoyed uninterrupted friendship with him. It was a life conversation that allowed them to know him without boundaries. To love him without limits. To *be* with him in uninterrupted intimacy. Only two people in history have ever been able to do that. Only two have ever known what life is like without disappointment. Without any pain or conflict. Without anxiety or insecurity. Or fear. Or concern about the future.

Imagine that.

Theirs was a world without negativity or sadness. They were the prototype male and female, made without fault, unblemished in body and in spirit. Designed to know God and enjoy him, they loved one another in their heaven on earth.

The Big Question

We don't know how long Adam and Eve were in Eden before things went south. But something happened to them then and there that still impacts us in the here and now. Something went wrong in the Garden of God that shattered their perfect world into 6 billion shards of sin.[4]

The man and woman were created, not *righteous*, as you might imagine, but rather, *innocent*, or free from the experiential knowledge of sin. They were also made in God's "image,"[5] meaning they possessed intellect, emotion, and the ability to choose, along with a huge capacity for morality, relationship, intimacy, and personal fulfillment.

The serpent in this story (Satan) was actually a former high-ranking heavenly angel previously known as Lucifer.[6] As part of his sentence for rebelling against God, he was cast down to earth. And God, for reasons that are not entirely known, permitted Satan to have access to the perfect couple he had made. This serpent did something no other creature had done before. At least none that we know of. This creature actually *spoke*, and there's no indication that Eve thought this was strange or uncommon. In any case, the snake's first words posed a very simple but pregnant question, and one meaningful enough to plant a seed of doubt in the beautiful woman's unstained brain. It was a doubt about God and the credibility of his word. A stealthy skepticism regarding his character, integrity, love, and ability to provide.

"Is God really *that* good?" the serpent asked slyly, his implication clear. "Could he be holding out on you? I mean, come on. Are you 100 percent sure he's being *good* to you? Really? *All* the time? Is he enough? Could there be something better? Something *more*?"

Eve immediately responded to the four-legged snake with the only answer she had in her repertoire: "God told us if we touch this tree or eat its fruit, we will die."

Good answer. But it didn't deter the serpent from his mission to devour her brain by filling it with his own tasty doubt and lies. He shot back more aggressively the second time, taking the gloves off. He was done with teasing and flirting. He now made a promise that he had no intention of keeping. He floated a lie her way to see what she'd do, knowing that sometimes the best deceptions aren't the "little white lies," but rather the big, bold, and brazen ones.

"You're not gonna die!" the serpent hissed, effectively insinuating, *The only thing that's going to happen is that you'll be elevated to a higher plane of consciousness. You'll get to know the things only God knows! Duh! You will be wise, just like him. And who wouldn't want that? He's been keeping you from experiencing all that life was meant to be. But I am doing you a favor by showing you the door to a better life.* "Trust me."

Convincing words. Served up like a plate of hot food to a hungry customer. Words spoken at the right time and with the appropriate vocal tone and inflection. The snake's claims, combined with the succulent, delicious-looking fruit staring Eve in the face, proved to be an irresistible combination. With her mouth watering, she plucked a piece of fruit right off the tree. And as soon as her pearly-white teeth sank into it, she instantly understood just what the serpent had been ranting about. It was everything she had hoped it would be, and more. So she offered it to her husband standing beside her, who was more than willing to partake in his first bite.

Then something unexpected happened, something Adam and Eve hadn't anticipated. Something they hadn't bargained for. And while the juices were still running down their chins . . .

. . . the virus kicked in.

The Naked Truth

Knowledge did come to the couple, just as the serpent had promised. He delivered on at least a portion of what he'd guaranteed. But it was the kind of knowledge for which they were very unprepared. The man and woman both realized they had committed the biggest *FAIL* in Earth's short history. They understood, for the first time, that they were naked. But no big deal, right? Agreed, unless your unclothed bodies now served as outward symbols of an inward and negative change. A one-of-a-kind, first-ever mutation had taken place only seconds earlier, in the blink of an eye. The physical consumption of the forbidden fruit reflected the couple's spiritual consent to ingest something far more deadly than a fig or an apple.[7] By eating what God had specifically told them not to, they had invited a lie into their unsoiled souls. They unlocked the front door and embraced an *untruth* about their God. And by doing what he explicitly forbade them to do, they had effectively cast him out of their lives. He wasn't good enough for them anymore. They had found something better. More appealing. More entertaining. More fun. Sound familiar?

Unfortunately, in doing so they had also inadvertently shut off their own air supply, disconnecting the flow of life to their souls.

They died inside.

And rigor mortis immediately began to set in, the foul stench of their inner corpses reaching their own nostrils. It was not a pleasant experience. *That's* why being naked was so embarrassing for them. And now you know. Adam and Eve's knowledge of evil baptized them into another consciousness altogether, immersing them into a whole new kind of world. The fallen kind. And because they had disobeyed God in their innocence, it would now become much easier to resist him in their fallen state. And easier to run from him. Which they did. It was futile to attempt to hide from the One who knows all things. In the game of hide-and-seek, he specializes in finding people who really don't care to be located. And once they're found, he's very good at redeeming them and restoring them, though for this to happen, there would be blood.[8]

But even redemption couldn't remove the sin virus now embedded deep within history's first couple. Included in this poison pill were some long-lasting side effects. For women, exponential pain in childbirth, along with an unnatural desire to rule over their husbands. For men, the sin-curse involved having to work the land in order to produce food, along with a chronic passivity. This gateway to darkness they had opened even caused creation itself to be affected by the invisible disease. And as for the serpent? He lost his legs in the deal, becoming cursed by God above all animals. Throughout history, Satan would despise humanity; knowing his execution date has already been set.

The man and woman were also banished from the garden where they once lived and loved. Yet even this punishment was a gracious provision from the God who still loved them. By keeping them out of the garden, he prevented them from eating from the Tree of Life, which would have locked them into a perpetual condemned state. But though God had cast them out of paradise, he had not personally rejected them forever.

It wasn't long after this that the man and woman had their first child. Unfortunately, the event didn't exactly produce the happy family they had hoped for. They initially had two sons (Cain and Abel), and I'm sure they prayed the ugliness that had stained their own souls wouldn't be passed on to their offspring.

It was not to be. It didn't take long for the very first baby born to begin showing signs of the evil passed on to him by his parents. And his inner zombie eventually took over. Following an argument with God in which the Lord warned him of the manipulative power of evil within him, Cain totally blew God off, refusing his help and advice. Motivated by jealousy, envy, and anger, the elder brother lured his younger sibling into the backyard and murdered him in cold blood. By taking the life of his only brother, Cain effectively killed one-fourth of the world's population. Humanity thus began a spiraled devolution into moral madness. And that's how this ancient evil found a home in the human heart. In your heart. And mine.

The spread of this virus also broke God's heart, so much so that he eventually said he was sorry he had ever made mankind.[9]

This sin virus is still 100 percent lethal and "heir"-borne, passed from parent to child in an unbroken chain of humanity.[10]

Currently 6 billion carriers worldwide.

Episode Two

ROTTEN TO THE CORE

Between being questioned and processed to make sure he wasn't infected, Ben phoned Crystal, and her roommate drove her downtown. After a long embrace, Ben assured her he was okay, and the two leaned against a squad car while crime scene investigators continued their work. In typical protocol, lights were set up and a white plastic barricade erected. Those examining the scene wore full-body hazmat suits, shielding them against any contamination or infection from the victim's blood. Ben still couldn't believe what had just happened to him.

• • •

It wasn't until the turn of the last century that the medical research community made tangible progress toward finding a cure for this virus that turns normal folk into maniacal flesh-eaters. By the late 1930s, a four-tiered stage had been mapped by German biophysicist Heinrich Von Zweig. Stage 1 includes ody. Dehydration becomes an obvious issue, but oddly, the individual rejects all forms of nourishment or hydration, even water. Stage 2 patients are required by law to check into government-run medical treatment facilities. These institutions became commonplace when then president Barclay pushed the National Regulatory Health Act through Congress. This bill created one hundred new treatment and containment facilities across the nation. And though most voters agreed something had to be done to treat those who fell victim to the virus, the bill also ignited a lot of controversy and opposition. One reason was because the president raised taxes to pay for construction of these new facilities. Subsequent protests and demonstrations prompted the president to respond with a nationally televised Oval Office address—now known as his "It's Now or Never" speech. In it, he applauded citizens for exercising their rights; however, he warned, "calculated measures must be taken to ensure that every American is free from this virus." He also repurposed thirty-five minimum-security prisons across the country, converting them into treatment and containment facilities. Thousands of criminals were relocated, forced into already overcrowded prisons.

Once admitted to a facility, the patient undergoes a wide battery of tests and treatments, including sedative medications, mental therapy, physical exercise, and even experimental drugs. Upon admittance, the patient's family is required to sign a waiver giving medical personnel freedom to use any means necessary for treatment. As expected, there's a lot of sadness during processing. Family members realize this is probably the last time they'll ever see their loved one alive. There is no return visit later to collect the body once he or she is deceased. The government takes care of that for you.

For health reasons, of course.

There are no cures for stages 1 and 2, though certain symptoms can be temporarily muted through strong pharmaceutical treatment.

While at the facility, the patient progresses to stage 3. Nausea and vomiting suddenly cease without warning. This previous sickness is replaced by a certain *madness*, accompanied by disorientation and loss of memory. The patient loses all recollection of who he is. Brain scans reveal little or no activity, and the salivary glands stop functioning. A blank, ghoulish gaze glazes across the eyes. The only thing the patient cares about is eating. Usually red, raw meat. As long as this patient, who by now is isolated from the rest of the facilities' population, can consume unprocessed and uncooked meat, he or she survives for a few weeks. But deny patients this gory delicacy and they fly into uncontrollable fits of rage. That leads to the final stage.

Stage 4 is the complete physiological and mental saturation of the Z-38 virus. Following the inevitable shutdown of the body due to lack of nourishment, death occurs. But only for a while. Within thirty minutes (sometimes sooner) the corpse reanimates. There is no detectable heartbeat or blood flow. The virus itself simply mutates and multiplies, strengthening the body to power up again. But though the cadaver comes back to life, it is clear that the person who once inhabited this corpse is long gone. Like some invisible internal battery, Z-38 facilitates movement for the soulless body. Gargling, moaning noises emerge from the vocal cords, and a rudimentary electrical impulse is detected in the brain.

A small percentage of stage 4 patients are kept in pits for observation and limited experimentation, but the vast majority are disposed of. The walking dead are lassoed and led to an outdoor corral or an underground bunker (depending on the facility) and shot.

Through the head.

"Cruel," some might say. Even "inhumane," perhaps. Well, it would be if these things were actually *human*. But these monsters have long since shed any vestige of humanity. What's left in every case is merely a rotting shell of flesh, bone, and muscle. Zombies can't be rehabilitated or redeemed. They aren't up for parole and they can't be changed. Ever. So it's not even a mercy killing. It's a necessary health act for national security.

The only effective way to take out a zombie is to hit 'em in the cranial cavity, every last one of them. Shoot them in the arms and torso all you want, and they'll keep coming. You have to go for the head. And no hand-to-hand combat either. Wielding an ax or swinging a baseball bat puts you at great risk for physical contact. One scratch. One cut. One bite. One bit of Z-38 from a zombie and it's *lights out* for you. Get wounded up close by one of these creatures, and you can sanitize and wash all you want, to no avail. This is serious business, with no room for misplaced bravado or unnecessary risk-taking. The stakes are way too high. These extermination crews shoot for accuracy and with definitive results. And you should, too, if you ever find yourself chased or cornered by one of these flesh-eaters.

• • •

After the authorities finished their questioning, Ben was free to go.

"I need pancakes," he announced to his girlfriend.

"Huh? What'd you say?" Crystal asked.

"Pancakes! I always eat pancakes when I'm stressed-out. Let's go to the Breakfast Shack."

"Sure, babe. Anything you say," she replied, putting an arm around her shivering boyfriend. It was the first cool day of fall, and temperatures in Corazon City were already into the 40s. Ben's only jacket was a thin hoodie.

"Do you mind driving? I'm still a little freaked-out," he said, tossing her his keys.

• • •

The Breakfast Shack is a restaurant frequented by Ben's age group. Located a few minutes' drive north of downtown, the stand-alone building is just off of Highway 89. The Shack is open 24/7, and Ben loves the old-school feel of the place.

The parking lot was empty that night, except for one 18-wheeler. Inside sat the lone trucker, parked at the counter. His cowboy hat was carefully perched on the stool beside him, like a loyal puppy waiting on his master. The man was finishing up a plate of bacon and eggs and working on his fourth cup of coffee. He casually turned and stared at the young couple who had just entered. Ben gave the trucker a nod as he and Crystal walked over to a corner booth and sat down. It was 11:45.

They hadn't been seated for ten seconds before two well-worn menus, stained with ketchup and syrup, fell from the sky, slapping onto the table in front of them.

"What'll you kids have to drink tonight?" the waitress said. Her name tag read, "Elvie," and as Ben looked at it, he silently mouthed the syllables to himself.

"It's pronounced 'EL-vee,'" the woman announced. Then, without waiting for the couple to answer, she produced two coffee cups and promptly filled them to the brim. "My momma and daddy were big fans of the King of Rock and Roll, and I was supposed to be a boy. You catch my drift?" she said, smiling to reveal a set of crooked, nicotine-stained teeth. Elvie looked about fifty, but was probably a lot younger. Ben guessed the waitress had lived a hard life. She could've easily climbed into that 18-wheeler outside and never skipped a beat.

"Nice to meet you, Elvie. I'm Ben, and this is Crystal."

"Pleasure to meet y'all too, sugar," Elvie replied.

"I haven't seen you here before," Ben said. "Are you new?"

"Honey, I've been here for three months. First shift, mostly," the waitress explained with a smirk.

"That's probably why," Ben concluded. "I don't usually come here till late at night. And we don't need menus. Just bring me your double stack and a big glass of milk."

"Just water for me. I'm not eating," Crystal quickly inserted.

"You got it," Elvie said, scooping up the menus. "SAM, GIMME A DOUBLE FLAPJACK!" she then yelled at the fry cook, who was standing only a few feet from her. The couple snickered, trying to hide their amusement at their new friend.

Ben took a deep breath and slowly exhaled, leaning back in the booth. Crystal reached across the table and took his hand.

"You okay? You're still shivering," she said quietly while looking over her shoulder at the trucker. The man slurped up the last of his black coffee and gave Crystal a wink while popping a toothpick in his mouth.

Ben stared at his girlfriend and swallowed hard.

"When I was a kid, my mom used to make me pancakes.

Big ones. Big as the plate," he said, a smile forming across his face. "I remember one day in second grade. Me and my older brother, Dan, were on our way to school—we walked to school because we lived real close. Anyway, we were late that day, and Mom rushed us out the door with a Pop-Tart in our hands. I dropped mine before making it to the sidewalk, and we ran all the way, just barely getting there on time. Dan outran me 'cause he was older and also the fastest kid in the fourth grade. I was out of breath and still laughing at some stupid joke Dan told. Anyway, I opened the door to my class and saw my principal sitting on a stool up front. Mr. Wingo. Big man. He kinda scared me 'cause he would always yell at you if you ran in the hallway. And I couldn't figure out why he was there, and I thought maybe I was in trouble for something.

"The rest of the kids were real still and quiet. Mr. Wingo looked at me, right at me, and said, 'Benjamin, come on in. Shut the door and take your seat, please.'

"I went straight to my desk and set my backpack on the floor. I didn't see my teacher, Miss Sullivan, and remember wondering where she was. I really liked her. She wasn't old and mean, like my first-grade teacher. Miss Sullivan was young and pretty, and she literally smiled all the time. If you ever got hurt on the playground, she'd hold you in her lap till you were better."

Ben smiled, taking a sip from his coffee. Crystal noted a distant look in his eyes. He continued.

"She was so . . . *nice.* Anyway, then Mr. Wingo said, 'Boys and girls, I am afraid I have some bad news. This morning on the way to school, Miss Sullivan was involved in an accident. Her car was hit by a big truck, and, well . . . Miss Sullivan . . . she's gone to be with God in heaven.'

"It took me a minute to get what he was saying. A bunch of kids started crying, and that pretty much was it. The door opened, and parents were already arriving. Mr. Wingo dismissed us from school. I grabbed my backpack, walked outside the room, and saw my mom in the hallway. I ran as fast as I could and grabbed her around the waist and cried.

"She took me home that day and made me the best pancakes I ever had. Steaming-hot buttermilk pancakes. With butter, hot syrup, and a glass of cold milk. I don't know why, but sitting in my mom's lap that morning, it . . . I just felt like everything was going to be okay. So sometimes when I get freaked-out, I just crave pancakes. Funny how things in your childhood mark you like that—for good *and* bad, I suppose. Anyway, isn't that just the stupidest thing you've ever heard in your life?"

"Not at all," Crystal said, tears filling her eyes. "I think it's the sweetest thing ever."

"So like tonight, when I walked up on that poor man. I don't know. I just panicked, I guess. It also brought back memories of when—"

"Ben," Crystal interrupted. "Don't, babe. Don't go there. Not tonight. You don't have to."

"I know, I know. It's just, when I saw him . . . ahh! Okay. Let's talk about something else, all right?"

Elvie returned, serving up a hot stack of pancakes and a glass of milk. "Here ya go, honey," she said, giving the cowboy trucker a wink as he walked out the door.

Ben unwrapped the silverware from the paper napkin, stared at his food, and then dug in, taking a huge bite.

I'm gonna go see my mom tomorrow, he thought to himself.

Chapter 2

THE DEPTH OF EVIL

The human heart is the most deceitful of all things, and desperately wicked. Who really knows how bad it is?

—**Jeremiah 17:9** NLT

What happened back at the dawn of creation was a train wreck. Humanity derailed and suffered a head-on collision with sin, and the result is . . . well, look at the world around you. Look at what we've become, at what humankind has done to itself. Look at your own city, school, or workplace, at the heartache suffered and lives forever mangled because of multiple train wrecks.

So how did we get from that original rebellion to where we are now? And what did we lose in this epic tragedy in the Garden? For one thing, we lost our once-transcendent health. Instead of enjoying a disease-free existence, our bodies now get sick and die. Can you imagine a world without runny noses, stomachaches, old age, and cancer? These are part of the death sentence we received for our act of treason against the Creator. We also lost our spiritual sensitivity to all things good. A tear appeared in the relationship fabric between God and us (and between one another). It tore top to bottom and left to right. Vertically and horizontally, producing a cross-shaped scar in every one of our hearts. Our dominion over nature was forfeited as well (Romans 8:19–22). Adam disqualified us all. Our perfect world was taken from us. Even the ground is cursed now (Genesis 3:17; Romans 8:19–22)!

But another lingering consequence from our spiritual stupidity is that the very image of God in us is marred almost beyond recognition. As a result, we don't function exactly like we used to . . . like we're *supposed* to. Things in us don't work right anymore. They do function, just not very well.

Whereas in the Garden the man and woman had a much greater capacity for thought, reason, creativity, and contemplation, now that capacity has been handicapped. Imagine having the mental creativity to name all the animals . . . off the top of your head! To comprehend the relationship between creation and its Creator. To think about God and life for an extended period of time. No attention deficit in the Garden. Imagine thinking deep thoughts about God. This doesn't mean that Adam and his bride had all knowledge, but just that their knowledge was unhindered, their thinking uninterrupted. Before the snake encounter, they also never had a single negative thought toward each other. Not one. Not a cross or critical word. No arguments or hurt feelings. And it never even occurred to them to disobey their Father or to stray from him. No psychological aberrance or disorders. Both Adam and Eve possessed beautiful minds. But be that as it was, our minds are now ruled by the flesh (our nature without Christ).[1] But our parents' Garden debacle goes beyond just brain damage. Another area affected by the famous fruit-picking incident was their *emotions*. Whereas before they were emotionally stable, after the fall they became more volatile and unsteady. Previously, their feelings weren't prone to rise and fall according to some invisible faulty inner thermostat. Emotionally, they were anchored. Reliable. Dependable. Secure. Happy. Pleased. Satisfied. Hopeful. Assured. Confident. Exhilarated. Peaceful. Grateful. Loving.

There was no sadness, disappointment, or depression. None. No boredom or apathy, anger or rage. No anxiety, stress, or confusion. Almost daily experiences for us, but not for Adam and Eve. They never experienced loneliness or rejection, remorse or guilt. No fear or panic. No embarrassment or jealousy. No suspicion or uneasiness. No envy or greed. No hostility or intimidation. No pressure. They never felt *used*. Never uncomfortable. There was no codependence or any sort of unhealthy feelings. Every emotion they possessed remained balanced, functioning like a smooth-running machine. It felt really good to be human.

A final area of our humanity impacted by this train wreck was our ability to choose. Don't misunderstand; we obviously still make choices. The difference is that the beauty and skill attached to an unstained soul is now gone. In its place, a downgraded version. All our choices after Eden became primarily motivated by a desire to please *self*. Our dominant trait became the absence of a desire to choose God. The prophet Isaiah wrote, "We all, like sheep, have gone astray, each of us has turned to his own way."[2]

Paul said nobody even seeks God.[3]

Surely you don't mean that, Paul! You make it sound like we're all bad *or something. Like we're evil. In reality, there are lots of good people who seek God. Right?*

Not exactly. Paul was saying that the curse within us is so corrupt that it causes us to reject anything remotely related to God. In our natural state, we simply don't like God very much. In fact, we really *dis*like him. A lot. His ways irritate and confuse us. His standards intimidate us. His timing frustrates us. He messes with our plans. He doesn't do things our way. He wants to be in charge of us. He says he deserves our undying praise. In fact, he demands it . . . all the time.

The *nerve*!

The "S Word"

In case you haven't noticed, most people aren't predisposed to running wildly toward this God. Instead, we default to running our own lives, thinking we can do a better job. Furthermore, we enjoy being in charge. We like answering only to ourselves. We want love, but love on our terms and as defined by us. We want patience and perseverance, but without pain and trouble. We want success, but no suffering. We want all the things God provides; we just don't want him, because he might mess things up.

It's sometimes subtle how we reject God.

That's who we *really* are, and that's why he calls us "sinners." Think about the word *sin*. It's one of those "Bible terms," and not one you overhear a lot at the local Starbucks. An archaic, nebulous word, it seems to change its meaning depending on the person using it. For some, sin is categorically defined by specific actions, such as going to an R-rated movie, drinking, dancing, listening to certain kinds of music, cussing, driving too fast, wearing short skirts, voting for the wrong political candidate, drinking caffeine, eating meat, or anything strictly prohibited by a particular religious group or church.

Fortunately for us, God doesn't simply give us a list of sins to avoid. There's a lot more to life (and to God) than spending our time watching out for all the "Don't" signs he's posted. He's much more concerned with our understanding of the concept of sin than he is with us making an A on the "No Sin" test. And though we commit individual "sins," sin itself is the evil principle that inherently dwells within us. It's more than some invisible disease we've acquired or a spiritual condition. It's actually a part of who we are. Inseparably intertwined in our spiritual DNA. It's as much a part of us as our gender or skin color, illegitimately encoded in us the moment our first parents bit into that fruit.

This word *sin* was originally used in ancient archery competitions. It simply meant "to miss the mark." To fail to hit the bull's-eye. So when God calls us *sinners*, he is saying we have missed the mark of his perfect standard. We don't hit God's "bull's-eye" of perfection. Ever. We don't measure up in character or in action. Our thoughts fall short. Our emotions are all over the target, our choices deliberately aiming at something else. We've come up short of the original idea he once had for his creation. We don't "make the cut." Scripture defines *sin* several ways: We sin by breaking God's revealed standards and laws. By refusing to believe God's Word. By asserting our will against his. By intentionally or unintentionally rebelling against him. Sin is both active rebellion and passive indifference. Action and attitude. Calculated pursuit of ungodliness as well as accidental unrighteousness. But sin's attachment goes even deeper. Beyond what we think, say, or do, we miss the mark. *We* are the problem.

This realization is precisely what led a great Christian like the apostle Paul to declare, "For I know that nothing good dwells in me, that is, in my flesh; for the willing is present in me, but the doing of the good is not."[4]

Have you made that same discovery about your own heart? Of course, compared to a serial killer, crooked politician, or drug-abusing rock star, you or I might look pretty righteous. But unfortunately for us, God doesn't put humanity in a big police lineup and pick out the bad guy over the other, lesser criminals. Instead, he measures us up against the standard of himself. He holds our character next to the brilliant glory of his pristine righteousness. And we come up short. Very short. Every time.

Episode Three

INTRUDER

At fourteen, Daniel Forman announced one evening at dinner, "Dad, I'm gonna be an FBI agent when I grow up."

"And I'm gonna be Spider-Man," young Ben countered sarcastically.

"Benjamin, don't mock your brother," his mother scolded. "He can be anything he wants to be."

"That's great, son," his dad responded, "but you've got plenty of time to make that decision."

"I'm serious, Dad. You'll see," said Daniel, confidently.

As he grew older, he was a natural athlete, and an above-average competitor. He enjoyed the physical contact of sports. But he was also a passionate hunter, often disappearing for days with friends into the nearby Smoky Mountains to wait out deer or track wild hogs. Dan loved firearms, and his bedside perpetually hosted a leaning stack of magazines on weaponry and warfare. Dan could take apart a pistol in about fifteen seconds, then reassemble it in thirty.

Upon reaching his growth peak, the eldest Forman boy

stood 6 feet tall and weighed 185 pounds. His short, brown hair; blue eyes; and chiseled jaw matched his intense spirit. Dan never did anything halfway. It was all or nothing with him.

Because of his passion for sports and the outdoors, there wasn't much time in Dan's life for serious romance. "Girls are high-maintenance," he declared. "Besides, football is my mission right now."

But Dan's driven personality was tempered by his love language: *protection*. For her birthday last year, he gave his mom a can of military-grade pepper spray. "It shoots a steady stream up to twenty feet. And it's ten times stronger than what the police use, Mom!" he excitedly announced as she unwrapped her present. Patricia Forman was expecting chocolates or a scarf. On Christmas Day he gave her a knife. A *knife*. Now, who gives their mom a knife for Christmas?

Dan Forman, that's who.

Following high school, he enrolled at Carolina Southern College to pursue a degree in criminal justice. But after four frustrating semesters, it became clear that academics weren't Dan's thing. Not that he wasn't intelligent. He just got bored with education. He'd rather *do* something than spend time reading about, as he put it, "things I'm never gonna use in life." So he punted college for something he could give his heart to, trading calculus for camouflage and enlisting in the Army. The military suited Dan more than college had. He preferred boots and ACUs to flip-flops and T-shirts. He loved the discipline and challenge of the military. He also enjoyed the camaraderie the Army fosters, of being a part of a special brotherhood.

But during Dan's third year in the Army, while stationed at Fort Bragg, something happened back home that deeply disturbed the young soldier. His parents, John and Patricia, were living in Corazon City, in the same house where Dan and Ben had grown up. Theirs was a modest three-bedroom, 1920s bungalow cottage in the "Old Town" district, and what's more, it was paid for. The Formans had always lived frugally, and since John was a handyman, he saved them thousands of dollars in repair work over the years. It was the only house the Formans had ever owned, and they took pride in making it the only *home* their boys would ever know.

"Boys need stability," John often said. "Family security is rooted in having a consistent home life, and that's why we're never moving from this place." As a result, Dan and Ben hardly knew a day when their dad wasn't home for dinner by 6 p.m.

John Forman was a man's man. An old-school guy. He liked traditional family values, sports, camping, and cooking out. And he loved his country. At Dan's football games, he'd often get emotional whenever "The Star-Spangled Banner" was sung. A gentleman, John Forman had little tolerance for any man who failed to open a door for a lady.

He'd met Patricia Kelly at age nineteen while attending a Corazon Mountaineers minor-league baseball game. Pat was working the concession stand that night. According to her, John kept returning to the stand, and by the end of the night, had consumed six hot dogs, four sodas, two bags of peanuts, and a candy bar. Finally, the teenage girl spoke up.

"Well, are you gonna ask me out on a date, or are you gonna keep eating and die of a heart attack first?" she asked.

And that began a friendship that grew into a courtship, with John finally popping the question in the fall of 1975. They were married the following spring, and after trying for eight years to have kids, they brought Daniel William Forman into the world, followed two years later by little brother Benjamin Charles.

At 6 feet, 2 inches tall and 235 pounds, John Forman was a barrel-chested man with a deep, booming voice, though he'd never been much for unnecessary words. Instead, he did most of his talking with his actions. "Hardworking Hoss Forman" (so-called by his friends) was a building inspector for Corazon County, overseeing all new construction. But come 5 p.m. each day, he'd leave with the same announcement: "See you people in the morning. John Forman is going home to eat the best cooking in Corazon City."

And that's where he was that Thursday afternoon, in the living room, dozing off in his favorite chair while Patricia finished up a batch of fried chicken, when suddenly, a mysterious man appeared in their entryway, walking through the Formans' front door as if it were his own home. John awoke to the sound of his wife's scream. Grabbing his glasses, he bolted out of his chair and ran into the front hallway. Once there, he instantly confronted the man, demanding that he leave. But the strange visitor simply stood there, glassy-eyed, hands dug deep in his pockets, staring in silence. Pat snatched her phone off the counter and called the police while John continued yelling at the man. But with no result. Within minutes, police arrived at the Forman residence and arrested the trespasser, who went quietly and without incident. Turns out he was a local vagrant. A little drunk or spaced-out perhaps, but harmless.

Afterward, John and Patricia laughed about the whole experience over a plate of lukewarm fried chicken. They called their boys, thinking they'd join them in seeing the lighter side of the situation. Both failed to see the humor, especially Dan, who was scheduled to come home that weekend.

"Dad," he scolded his father over the phone, "you were unprepared! I'm really disappointed in you. That guy could have been armed, or a *killer*. You left your door unlocked and your home unprotected. You were vulnerable and put Mom at unnecessary risk. You just can't afford to do that these days. We'll talk more about this when I get home. Bye!"

And the phone went dead.

"Pat," John said to his wife with a smile, "I think I'm in trouble with our son."

● ● ●

When Dan arrived home that Friday, Ben joined them for a much-anticipated family reunion. By special request, Patricia cooked her boys their favorite meal—meatloaf with twice-baked potatoes, macaroni and cheese, corn on the cob, and chocolate pie. Once supper was over, Ben retreated to the TV room. Meanwhile, Dan produced a "dummy" handgun from his duffel bag, then proceeded to lead his parents on a room-by-room sweep of his boyhood home, demonstrating at every doorway how to properly clear a room without getting shot.

"Now, Dad, *you* do it," he said, handing the realistic-looking gun to his father. Obliging his enthusiastic firstborn, John stealthily moved from kitchen to den to bedroom, peering around corners like a TV detective, Dan instructing along the way.

"That's it, Dad. Now you're getting the hang of it."

When they finished, the three returned to the living room. Dan shut off the TV (irritating Ben) and reached again into his duffel bag, this time revealing a small package.

"Here, Dad," he said, handing it to him. "This is for you."

John opened the box, and to his surprise saw a Springfield 1911, .45-caliber handgun inside.

"It's got an eight-round magazine. I want you to keep it nearby at all times in a secret but accessible location. Tomorrow morning, we're going to the shooting range, and I'm gonna show you guys how to handle it properly. Ben, you can come too. In fact, you should," Dan said matter-of-factly.

Ben, still irritated from having his TV watching interrupted, responded, "No thanks, bro. I'm good. But you guys knock yourselves out."

"Suit yourself," Dan replied.

"Son, this is all very nice, but you really didn't need to go out and buy me a gun," John said, chuckling.

"Dad! Come on. This is serious business. I can't be here to look after you guys, so you're gonna have to be more alert from now on."

John Forman's gray hair didn't simply mean he was getting old. There was also a healthy dose of wisdom within those silver locks of his. The fifty-six-year-old could tell how much this meant to his son. And as a father, it struck a chord deep inside. He realized Dan was only trying to say, "I love you, Mom and Dad, and I don't want to lose you."

John looked at the man standing before him. As a boy, Dan had loved helping his dad with projects out in the back shed—handing him tools, holding the wood while he sawed, and helping clean up afterward. And if John hit his finger or got a splinter, Dan was quick to respond.

"Mom! Dad's hurt. I gotta get a Band-Aid, quick! He needs me!"

Dashing out the back door, he'd leap down the steps, running to his dad's rescue. And whether he needed the Band-Aid or not, John always put it on. Dan just wanted to help. And protect. He still does.

Like most dads, John wished he could turn back the clock and have one more day with his sons at home. Even so, he had a treasure chest of memories. He had done his best to make men out of his boys, and for Dan, the Army had nearly perfected that process. Now his little helper was a grown man.

John knew just what to say to his eldest boy. He always did.

"Son, I know. I get it. I really do. Your mom and I sincerely appreciate what you're doing. And I promise you, I will be more alert . . . just like you say."

The next morning, the three of them went to the shooting range. Make that four, as Ben made a last-minute decision to accompany his family.

• • •

Late one Saturday afternoon the next summer, John was out in the shed, refinishing an old table he had found at a garage sale earlier that day. It would be a surprise gift for Patricia, who loved old furniture. Suddenly he heard an unfamiliar noise behind him. Turning toward the shed's double wooden doors, John squinted over his reading glasses to see the outline of a man silhouetted by the setting sun. As the figure stepped closer, John was horrified to discover a reanimated male zombie lumbering straight toward him!

Forman froze. Ever since Dan's visit, John had been diligent to carry his .45 pistol with him to the shed whenever he was alone, just in case. But not today. All his good intentions and previous diligence meant nothing in this moment. He had unloaded the table into the shed that morning without coming inside the house. In his excitement to make a gift for his bride, a gun had been the furthest thing from his mind.

John frantically looked around the workshop and grabbed the first thing his hands touched, a quart-sized can of varnish. He hurled the container at the beast. It bounced off and rolled down the driveway. Patricia heard the noise and glanced out the kitchen window, puzzled at why a can of varnish would be tumbling down her driveway. Then her eyes diverted toward the shed, and it took her all of three seconds to figure out what was happening.

This zombie was barefoot, with disheveled hair tangled

in dried blood. Through his torn shirt, she could see flaps of rotted flesh hanging from his torso. Patricia Forman was instantly covered with a blanket of fear.

"Dear God in heaven, help me!" she said in a quivering voice. Shocked and confused, she wondered, *Should I get the gun first or call the police?* Acting on sheer impulse, she frantically dialed 999, the dedicated emergency number established for any confirmed zombie sighting. She gave her address to the response specialist, and a team was dispatched at once. But there wasn't time to wait on them. She ran to the bookcase in the den and reached for the books John used to conceal his weapon, violently jerking them off the shelf.

Meanwhile, her husband and best friend for more than thirty years was cornered in his workshop shed, with nowhere to go and nothing but empty space between himself and a hungry monster. John was overcome by the sudden, putrid smell of rotting flesh. His eyes darted around the shed, looking for some weapon to fend off the approaching beast. Reaching for a nearby crowbar, he gripped the cold steel with both hands, like a baseball bat. He then hurled it with all the force his large frame could muster. The heavy steel object propelled end over end toward the loudly groaning zombie, striking his shoulder with the sharp end and removing a hunk of dead flesh.

Staggering, but only slightly deterred, the monster kept coming, more determined now. With nowhere to run, John Forman calmly reached behind him and retrieved a large screwdriver from off the wall. Gripping it tightly in his right hand, he set his stance and waited for the inevitable.

Chapter 3

THE TWO YOUS

The old nature will never give up; it will never cry
truce; it will never ask for a treaty to be made between
the two . . . What a fight.

—**Charles Spurgeon**

My heart is half devil and half beast.

—**George Whitfield**

The War Within

It happened one night following a meeting where I had
spoken.

She wove through the crowd, making her way toward me.
Twenty-four-year-old Amber was in tears by the time she got
to me. Eyes red and puffy, with mascara running down her
cheeks. I thought someone had died, so I quickly walked her
over to the side where we could talk more privately.

"So, what's up? What's going on?" I asked.

"It's terrible, and I just don't understand it," she said. "For
years, I've thought I was a Christian, but now I'm not sure anymore. There's no way I can be."

"Tell me what makes you say that, Amber."

"It's the constant frustration I face every day. I wake up

ready to follow God, but by lunch I've done something stupid. I think and do things that real Christians don't do. Then I feel bad and tell him how sorry I am. And everything is good for a while, but then I do it again. But that's the thing. I don't want to! I don't want to disappoint God. I want to please him, and sometimes I do. But then I screw up again!"

"Okay," I said. "And you feel like that makes you an unbeliever?"

"Well, duh! People who love God don't sin like me! You don't understand. It's not just that I slip up. I actually *want* to do those things. I consciously choose to. But in my heart, I really *don't* want to. But I do! But I don't *want* to! Aaaaaaah!"

Tears continued flowing as she unsuccessfully attempted to wipe them away.

"I see. And coming to realize you're not a Christian after all these years would be a hard pill to swallow. And bad news, for sure. But can I share another possible scenario with you? According to Scripture, it just may be that your frustrating internal struggle proves just the opposite. In all the years I've been in ministry, I haven't known many non-Christians who have experienced the roller-coaster experience you have described. They simply do what pleases them, without thinking about whether it's wrong or offensive to God. And they usually don't feel that guilty afterward, confessing their sin to God. They also aren't so sensitive to Christ that they weep uncontrollably over their disloyalty to him. Amber, your sin-struggle only confirms that you really are a Christian. And a pretty sensitive one, at that."

After we looked at Scripture and prayed together, Amber walked away that night renewed and encouraged. She had hope. Not from me, but from God. She left with the knowledge of what he says about her identity and the war within. Her ability to move forward hinged on her accepting God's

The Two Yous

thoughts instead of her own. She now knew that even her emotions couldn't be trusted.

Amber is not alone in her confusion. Every God-worshipper from biblical times until now has experienced this madness. Though not every Christian may suffer the extent of Amber's doubt, they still deal with the same frustration and confusion. Most do question the reality and validity of their faith from time to time. And that can be a healthy exercise. But every one of us deals with the identical battle. Amber's struggle had to do with controlling her anger and forgiving others. Your battleground may lie in another area—like promiscuity, homosexuality, lust, Internet porn, drunkenness, drugs, hate, misuse of money, gambling, gluttony, self-abuse, food addictions, or some other specific sin. The point is that it's a common struggle for all of us. We're all sinners.[1] But depending on our backgrounds, previous experiences, personalities, and personal weaknesses, our temptations may differ.

Second, the war within you is ongoing. Physical wars rarely end in a day, or a month or a year. Battle campaigns are complicated and complex. This, along with a brilliantly hidden enemy, dictates that ground troops are forced to fight in prolonged military campaigns. It's not clean, casualty-free, or quick. Instead, it's messy, deadly, and drawn-out.

A Corpse at the Core

The spiritual war within is similar to this and won't be over until the Prince of Peace returns or until we go see him at death. Until then, there is conflict, confusion, sin, victory, loss, wounds, pain, and scars. And a zombie living inside you.

It's the living dead within. A rotting spiritual corpse left over from your former self. It takes part of its identity from the person you were before you became a Christian. Some

Christians have a "before and after" story of conversion that includes some pretty dramatic escapades. But if you trusted Christ at an early age, you may have some difficulty seeing yourself as a former "child of Satan." I mean, how bad can a five-year-old be? It's not like you were doing drugs, sleeping around, or robbing convenience stores. Nevertheless, the Bible says that you were born with the same rotten, sinful nature as everyone else.[2] What's more, as we grow and mature, that old nature—sometimes called "the flesh," "self," the "old man," or the "sin nature"—continues decaying and rotting in its character.[3] Just like a zombie.

It never gets better. Only worse. More sinful. More wicked. More grotesque. More vile. More detestable. Thing is, this zombie goes with you wherever you go. Not always visible or vocal, but it is still there. With you at school, on the job, hanging with friends, at the dinner table with family, on a date, in a meeting, on the playing field, in the locker room, and when you're alone at night in your room. It never leaves you because it *is* you. Or a part of you.

And it knows you well—your tendencies, habits, patterns, thoughts, and weaknesses. It's had all your life to study and mold you. And it lives for nothing more than to turn you away from your Savior. If it can't do that, it will draw you into a lifestyle of self-pleasure. And if it can't do that, it will lull you into becoming religious, trading in spirituality for self-serving, consumer-driven Christianity. But therein lies the deception. Catering to self—whether it's in church or in the world—is still self-worship.

That's just one way this sinful nature inside influences you. It influences your mind, emotions, and will. Your friendships, relationships, family decisions—everything.

You soon become frustrated with yourself. Upset. Confused. Wondering why a Christian would have this much trouble following God. Other Christians seem to be doing fine, or at least much better than you. This creates doubt, leading to more confusion. You question your faith, your maturity, and like Amber, even your salvation. You wonder which one is the real you and which one is the imposter. You feel totally comfortable with being both the new you and the old you—depending on your mood or circumstances. Sometimes you feel so close to God that it takes your breath away. Then other times (possibly just minutes later) you find yourself embracing the very sin you hate. And you get this brain glitch thing in your head that goes something like this: *Wait! Just a little while ago I was talking about Jesus and loving God and feeling like life couldn't get any better. And now I'm totally into this sin. I'm doing something I know makes God sad. But that's really not me. But I'm still really loving it. But not really. I love God, not sin. But I'm not really wanting to love him right now, and I feel guilty about that. But not so guilty that I'm gonna stop. Gosh! This is crazy! How am I supposed to make any sense of this? How do I make sense of me?!*

A First Step in a Long Journey

This internal irritation won't go away. It's deeply disturbing. And embarrassing. It makes you feel like a fake. It confounds your understanding. And you wonder if you have some weird form of "spiritual schizophrenia." If you've ever felt like that, don't hit the panic button yet. After knowing Jesus for more than twenty years, Paul wrote, "I decide to do good, but I don't really do it; I decide not to do bad, but then I do it anyway . . . I've tried everything and nothing helps. I'm at the end of my rope. Is there no one who can do anything for me?"[4] That doesn't sound like a man who has his act together. It's not the journal entry of a baby believer, or someone who doesn't understand

Jesus, the Bible, or theology. This guy wrote half of the New Testament! He *gets* it. Paul had walked a long path with Christ. He had many years under his belt. He suffered enormously for the gospel.[5] He was a seasoned veteran. An experienced warrior. A future Hall of Famer. A pioneer missionary-pastor.

But he was still a man. A sinner with a sin nature like yours. So isn't it somewhat reassuring that someone as great and as greatly used by God as Paul experienced the same annoying struggle that you do? He fought in an ongoing battle with temptation and slavery to sin. Like us, he had an enemy within. A soul zombie bent on sabotaging his relationship with God. Paul knew what it feels like. And it broke his heart because he also loved Jesus more than anything.

But what does it mean to say, "What I want to do, I don't do," and, "What I *don't* want to do, I end up doing anyway"? It makes it seem as if your life is out of control. And in your worst moments you ask yourself, "How can I be so sinful?" The answer is, of course, that you have a zombie inside you. Once alive and normal in the Garden, human nature was reanimated into a hideous creature. It lives to devour your mind, and given the chance, will attack and destroy you. It won't go away just because you throw Bible verses at it. And because as a Christian you now have the Holy Spirit also living in you, a true holy war has been declared within.[6] Some have described this experience as a "tug-of-war," but it goes way beyond simply being pulled one way or another. It's more than just who's going to tug at you today—the Holy Spirit or your old sinful nature. It's a life-and-death struggle. An epic battle between good and evil, flesh and Spirit, and your heart is the valley of decision. It's about desire, control, and life. The Spirit gives life, and the flesh takes it away.

But every journey begins with one step. And ours is to recognize the sin nature's presence and power. It would be naive to deny this dark reality, or to ignore its long-standing reign in your life. Its root system extends deep beneath the surface of who you are. Dig up one root, and another one appears. And while you're uprooting that one, the first one grows back. This eventually leads you into a frustrating cycle of failure, guilt, confession, repentance, trying harder, failure, guilt, confession, and so on and so on.

And who wants to live like that?

Not Amber.

Not me.

How 'bout you?

Episode Four

FUNERAL FOR A ZOMBIE

Patricia Forman hit the back door running, nearly taking it off its hinges. Racing down the porch steps, her five-foot-four, petite frame pulsed with adrenaline as she sprinted toward the wooden shed, the large handgun held tightly in her hands. She had handled it only one other time—that day at the shooting range with Dan. Stopping fifteen yards shy of the shed, she took careful aim, with feet firmly planted, and began firing. The bullet's blast echoed across the neighborhood, and her first three shots missed wildly to the right. The pistol's recoil, combined with Patricia's trembling hands, guaranteed further misses unless she corrected herself. She paused, focused her sight, and fired once more, striking the zombie in the lower back. The bullet hit with a muffled thud, sending hollow-point fragments scattering inside his decaying torso. Unfortunately, it did nothing to stop him. However, the fifty-five-year-old woman was gradually harnessing her adrenaline to her advantage. The next two bullets caught the walking dead man in the shoulder. Side-by-side shots. A four-inch-wide section of his left shoulder blade instantly disintegrated. Patricia's confidence and accuracy were growing with every pull of the trigger.

John had a limited view of his wife, who was off to his right. "In the *head*, Pat! You have to hit him in the *head*!" he shouted.

"Lord," she prayed, "if only Dan was here. Help me, Father!"

The zombie lunged at her husband. She fired once more, hitting him in the neck, removing a large section of it. The flesh-eater stiffened and paused briefly, turning his head toward the small woman, grinding his dulled, black teeth at her. Then, as if nothing had happened, he resumed pursuit of his prey.

Patricia took a deep breath and stared intently down the gun's barrel. And just as her son had taught her months earlier, she exhaled, gently squeezing the trigger. The eighth and final round exploded out of the barrel, rocketing toward the zombie at eleven hundred feet per second.

The projectile struck him behind the left ear, severing it from his rotting body.

Her magazine was now empty; nevertheless, Patricia kept squeezing the trigger, hoping somehow there might be another bullet. *One more shot*, she thought. *I know I can hit him this time!*

But the gun was empty. She was out of bullets.

Back in the shed, John tightened his grip on the large screwdriver and—going on the offense—took a deliberate step forward and plunged the full length of the nine-inch shank deep into the zombie's skull. Simultaneously, the zombie bent forward and sank his poisoned teeth into Forman's shoulder.

"AAAAGGHH!"

John let out a painfully loud groan, gnashing his teeth together in unimaginable agony. The zombie bit again, ripping out a mouthful of flesh.

"PAAAT! Pat! I love you!" he called out in a trembling voice.

It was the only time she'd ever seen her strong husband show fear.

Just then Pat heard another voice, this one from behind.

"Get down, Mrs. Forman! On the ground! NOW!" Two police officers had arrived and with guns drawn were sprinting down the long driveway. The zombie pivoted toward the shed's opening, still chewing a piece of John's flesh.

BOOM!!

The first officer dropped the zombie with one shot through his decomposing forehead, sending bone and flesh fragments flying against the back wall. He was dead. This time for good.

The second officer stepped up and drew a bead on Forman himself, taking precise aim for the kill shot. John held his shoulder, trying to impede the flow of blood ebbing between his fingers. Turning his gaze toward the policeman, he instantly recognized him. Officer Grant Tanner knew the Forman family well, having played high school football with their son Dan. Mr. Forman had taken Dan and his football buddies on camping trips and hosted numerous postgame pizza parties at their house. The two men locked eyes. Both were sweating and breathing heavily, one from shock and impending death and the other from pure adrenaline.

"This is *not* good," the twenty-five-year-old mumbled under his breath. As a trained responder, he was well aware that in a matter of minutes, John Forman would no longer be *John Forman*. He knew the virus was now racing through Forman's veins, and that the transformation had already begun. He also knew that his life and the lives of everyone in that neighborhood would be in grave danger if he didn't pull that trigger and drop Forman right where he stood. A hot bead of sweat navigated its way down the middle of his back. This was his first zombie encounter as a young police officer.

Patricia stood twenty feet to Tanner's immediate left. She turned toward the man who had shared countless meals at the Forman dinner table.

"Grant . . . listen to me," she calmly pleaded. "You know us! Please, for God's sake, don't do this!"

Tanner's mouth went dry as he found himself locked inside a moral and personal dilemma. This was a no-win situation. No matter what his decision, there would be no happy ending to this story. His mind told him to simply do his job and take the shot. But his heart longed to spare the man who had shown so much kindness to him years ago. Tanner was already feeling guilty for what he was about to do. But this was no time for sentimentality. It was a time for duty. Grant Tanner had raised his right hand and taken a solemn oath to defend the citizens of Corazon City against any and all threats to public health or safety.

The officer reset his stance, placing his finger on the trigger.

John Forman looked once more at his bride. His mind traveled back to that night at the ball field where he saw her for the first time. He thought, *She's just as beautiful today as she was then.*

John wished he could tell her that.

He knew this was the last time they would see each other in this life. He exhaled a sigh of resignation, then gave Tanner a nod. It was his final act of sanity, as the virus was fast taking effect. Pat closed her eyes. Tanner hesitated no longer. His training kicked in, and he fired two precision shots, killing the soon-to-be zombie stone-cold dead where he stood. John's body slumped to the shed's concrete floor, coming to rest beside the twice-dead ghoul. Patricia dropped to her knees, releasing the still-warm gun onto the manicured lawn. She began to weep uncontrollably. More sirens wailed as containment specialists arrived to begin cleanup and removal of the bodies.

• • •

Four days later, John was buried at Forest Lawn Cemetery. Family and friends packed out Pine Valley Community Church, where the Forman family had attended for years. Following the graveside service, close friends and relatives descended on the Forman home. Ben and Dan found themselves in the house, surrounded by people.

Finishing a bite of chicken salad, Dan remarked, "Before I left for college, Dad said that if anything ever happened to him, there would be some life insurance money coming our way. I don't mean to sound insensitive, but I think we should discuss it. You and me are all Mom has now. I don't know how much money we're talking about, but once this funeral stuff is behind us, we're gonna sell the house. Then I propose we use the money to buy some land and build a new place for Mom, somewhere away from here."

Ben put down his drink and looked around to make sure no one was hearing their conversation.

"Can we talk about this outside?" he said, motioning toward the backyard. The two Forman boys maneuvered their way through the crowd toward the back door, but not before pausing to hug well-meaning friends and distant relatives. And with every hug came the awkward, obligatory comments.

"We're sure gonna miss him, Ben."

"Great service, Dan. What you said really touched my heart."

"One thing for sure, he loved his boys."

"He was a good man."

"If there's anything we can do, you just call us, honey," Aunt Lola said, planting a lipstick-smudged kiss on Ben's cheek.

Finally, they made it safely to the back patio.

"Whew. I'm sure glad that's over," Ben exclaimed, wiping lipstick off of his cheek.

"Seriously," Dan said, chuckling. "Now I know why they're called 'distant relatives.' You wanna keep your distance from them!"

This produced a laugh. It had been days since either of

them had smiled. The grief was understandably overwhelming for the boys. They'd spent their entire lives idolizing their dad. Still reeling from the shock of his death, each would have to deal with that devastating loss in his own way. Ben stuffed the lipstick-stained napkin into his coat pocket, scanning the backyard where both of them had grown up.

"Dad taught me how to ride a bike down this driveway. I plowed headfirst right into that bush," he said, pointing. "Still have a scar under my eyebrow." Ben felt the scar with his finger. "And how 'bout all those birthday parties Mom threw for us back here?"

"Dad threw the football to me every afternoon the summer before my junior year. Fifteen minutes before supper. Every night. He never complained, though I know it must have hurt his arm. I ran a slant pattern too long a few times and flipped right over the chain-link fence. I just knew one day I'd play in the NFL," Dan said, shaking his head. He took a long drink from the punch-filled paper cup, staring at the backyard grass that held so many memories. Then his jaw tightened, and he crushed the empty cup in his hand. Ben had seen that look on Dan's face countless times growing up. It usually meant his big brother was about to hit something, and usually it was *him*! But this was different. Dan was definitely angry, but this time his rage was directed within.

He spoke slowly through his teeth.

"I wasn't there, Ben. I couldn't protect them this time."

"Don't do this to yourself, Dan. What happened here wasn't your fault and you know it. It's not fair," Ben said, attempting to comfort his big brother.

"If I had just spent more time showing Mom how to use the gun. I know she would have been able to—" Huge tears were now silently rolling down his cheeks.

Ben interrupted his brother. "Hey, look at me!" he said

54

firmly. "We can't change the past or spend our lives second-guessing. It was Dad's *time*. You've said it before, about guys in combat, remember? 'When it's your time, there's nothing you can do about it. You just hope you die well.' Those are your words. Dan, our father did that. He died well."

"I know. I *know*, Ben! But this time it's . . . it's different. Never mind. Just forget it, okay?"

The brothers stood in an awkward quiet, the silence broken by the sounds of summer birds.

Then Ben summoned the courage to speak.

"Look at all the memories we have here. We have to remember the great childhood Dad gave us. That's why we can't sell this place. This is Mom's *home*. We have to think about her now."

"I *am* thinking about Mom! And that's exactly why we have to sell it. Without Dad here, she's gonna be all alone. Her greatest need isn't sentimentality now. It's *security*. What's more, there's no way she can keep up an old house like this. Too many repairs and things that could go wrong. Besides, now there's also some really sad memories, ya know?"

"I see what you're saying. I do," Ben replied. "But the thought of this place not being in the family anymore just . . . I don't know. I'm not sure it's a good idea just yet."

The clanging of plates rattled through the open kitchen window, and that meant Patricia Forman was already busy with cleanup. Within a minute, she appeared at the back door, drying her hands on a familiar dishrag. Descending the steps, she paused to give a disturbing glance toward the old shed.

"So, what are you boys doing out here? Being unsociable?" A tone of correction colored her voice.

"Oh no," they said, virtually in unison, with Dan adding, "We were just . . . uh . . . getting some fresh air. Right, Ben?" he prodded, with an elbow to his brother's ribs.

"Yep, that's what we're doing. Fresh air."

"Uh-huh," Patricia said, unconvinced. "Well, no matter. Just gives me an excuse to come out here and be with you two."

The three of them stood there in the backyard while guests continued mingling inside.

"Momma?" Ben addressed her as if he were sixteen again.

"Yes, baby, what is it?" she said.

Dan suspected his brother would bring up the house issue. He caught his eye and slowly shook his head.

Ben paused, staring at the grass. Then he looked up, tears clouding his vision. "Momma, I was just thinking. They just don't make men like Dad anymore, do they?" His voice quivered.

Patricia Forman's shoulders slumped. After stuffing the old dishrag into her apron, she reached up and placed a hand on each of her boys' cheeks.

"Oh yes they do," she said confidently. "And I'm looking at two of them right now. Your daddy was so very proud of his boys." She paused, then said, "Do you remember our trip to the Grand Canyon and the family picture we took there? Not long ago, I caught your daddy standing by the fireplace, staring at that picture.

"'Pat,' he said, 'God must really love us to have given us such wonderful sons.'"

Patricia lovingly kissed her boys, and the three enjoyed a long embrace. Dan whispered into his mother's ear, "If one day I could just be half the man he was."

"You are, sweetheart," she whispered back. "You are."

Standing in the backyard that afternoon, Dan decided there was going to be a big change in his life.

Chapter 4

DEEDS OF THE FLESH

Commit the oldest sins in the newest kind of ways.

—**Shakespeare, from** *Henry IV*

From the Inside Out

The Pharisees were the Jewish religious leaders of Jesus' day. But they were also masters at making up rules and twisting God's standards to suit their own purposes. We'll get to know these guys better a little later. However, in one scene out of Jesus' life, he was correcting the Pharisees' teaching that the things of this world "contaminate" us. Apparently his disciples weren't getting the concept, prompting Jesus to call them dull.

Nice.

Specifically, Christ was speaking of eating certain foods, which the Pharisees said made you "unholy." He was teaching, though, that external practices don't possess the ability to make us holy or unholy, righteous or evil. Physical things can't change anything about us spiritually—for bad or good.

In other words, we're not unblemished little children who play outside and happen to fall into a mud puddle, thus staining ourselves. He said that our filthiness begins in our hearts.

The things that make us dirty come from within. From the heart. We are, in reality, "sin factories," churning out an assembly line of iniquity. Culture, media, people, and the Internet may promote ideas and temptations our way. They may prompt us to sin, but they can't force us or produce it inside us. It doesn't mean they're harmless; it just means we can't lay the blame for our sin at their feet. To infer that our sin problems are a result of the "big, bad world" out there is to defy the very words of Jesus. If you check out Mark 7:13–23 in your Bible, you'll see a pretty serious list of things that Jesus said flow out of the human heart. And there's no doubt that they're all out there in society. However, literally every one of them has its genesis in the human heart.

Paul expanded on this idea while writing to his Galatian friends. He understood that once sin is conceived in our minds or manufactured in our hearts, it is then birthed in actions. Though he did not intend to produce an exhaustive list, he did give us some of the biggies: "The acts of the flesh are obvious: sexual immorality, impurity and debauchery; idolatry and witchcraft; hatred, discord, jealousy, fits of rage, selfish ambition, dissensions, factions and envy; drunkenness, orgies, and the like. I warn you, as I did before, that those who live like this will not inherit the kingdom of God."[1]

Paul actually separated these sin acts into groups for us so we could better understand them. They fall into the categories of sexual, spiritual, and social sins. Let's identify them individually so we can recognize them better.

Sex Sells

Sexual immorality, impurity, and debauchery. The first word Paul used was *porneia*. Doesn't take a linguistic genius to figure out what word we get from that. Paul was referring to the desire within our hearts to seek and experience sexual fulfillment outside of God's awesome design. This included things like adultery, premarital sex, homosexuality, bestiality, and incest. Paul was dealing with an extremely pagan culture. There was just one church, and it met in somebody's home. One church in Corinth. One in Ephesus, and so on. So Christianity hadn't yet made a huge impact on the moral code and consciousness of society. In a Roman world, pagan cult temples were in abundance and encouraged the exploration of virtually every kind of sexual experience. Temple prostitutes were common, and Christians coming out of that culture had no doubt once paid their "tithe" in a pagan temple in order to have sex with one of those prostitutes. That was considered an "act of worship" to their god. But that wasn't the worst of it. Paul even had to remind the Corinthian Christians to deal severely with one of their members who was sleeping with his stepmom![2]

We can never underestimate the wickedness of the human heart. It's capable of causing a person to perform unspeakable acts. And that includes believers in Jesus. Given the right circumstances, nothing is out of bounds or off-limits when it comes to our sin nature. And this is especially true concerning our sexuality. We live in a culture that encourages us to keep our sexual options open, allowing our desires and fantasies to be fulfilled.

Impurity is a broad term that refers to anything that is not *pure*, sexually speaking. That sounds simplistic, but it was intended to be understood that way. Though the word can mean literal physical uncleanness, it is often used specifically of sexuality.[3] You could apply it to anything that makes the Holy Spirit inside you uncomfortable. That extends to those areas of sexuality not clearly addressed in Scripture. What might that be for you?

Debauchery isn't a word we use every day, is it? Sounds like something you might have heard the Pilgrims or the Puritans say. Sometimes translated "sensuality," *debauchery* means "an unbridled lust or excessive, outrageous sexual behavior." Jesus mentioned this one in Mark 7:22 (translated "lewdness"). Paul also encouraged the Romans to drop this activity from their behavior repertoire.[4] *Debauchery* just means things have gotten out of control for you, sexually. That typically happens in relationships somewhere in that vast expanse between holding hands and crawling into bed.

Those are some of the sexual acts our dark hearts desire to do. And let's just be honest here. Sex is among the most potent "narcotics" known to man. And God designed it that way. He invented sex. But he also intended it to go way beyond just a physical experience. Sex connects two people emotionally and relationally. Even spiritually. I suspect Paul began his catalog of sin-nature deeds with sexual sins because the Christians in his culture were very familiar with them and would immediately understand what he was talking about. And so do we. All of these originate in the heart.

A Different Kind of Spiritual "High"

Paul mentioned just two spiritual sins: idolatry and witch-craft. Again, prominent in his world, and in ours. *Idolatry* means more than carving out a little god statue to worship and display on the fireplace mantel. These days an idol isn't something before which you physically bow down. An idol is anything or anyone that you place above God in your life. It's something that you give preference to *over* God. You're more loyal to it. More faithful. There's an attachment and allegiance associated with it. So we can make idols out of possessions, like cars, iPhones, guitars, or laptops. Idols can be music, bands, education, hobbies, jobs, or a career. Or even people—anything that rises above our desire for God.

The Greek word for *witchcraft* that Paul used was *pharmakeia* and refers specifically to drugs used in the practice of sorcery and witchcraft. In those days, *sorcery* referred to any practice that attempted to *connect* the living with departed humans or demonic spirits, or to *protect* someone from them. A witch or sorcerer would often use various drugs, accompanied by incantations or spells, as he or she appealed to supernatural powers.

A few years back, a witchcraft shop opened in my neighborhood. The shop sold a wide selection of books on the occult, witchcraft, and wizardry. Amulets and charms, along with an entire wall of potions, were sold to help the buyer cast spells. There were also pamphlets on paganism, teaching the reader how to listen to and hear from demonic spirits. But I didn't see any drug-related literature or paraphernalia (you had to go to the shop next door to get that stuff). On my several visits to the witch shop, I spoke with the owner and discovered that she had moved from another country specifically to open this store in our area, and that it was a literal "mission" of sorts, opened for the purpose of spreading paganism. It lasted a few years and then went out of business.

Paul, in his list of spiritual sins, chose to combine this drug-filled witchcraft (*pharmakeia*) with idolatry because of its partnership with the pagan religions of his day. *So*, you may be thinking, *I totally get the modern-day idolatry thing. But is witchcraft really a temptation for most believers today?* Great question, and the simple answer is, "Not exactly." But part of the spiritual relationship between *pharmakeia* and idolatry may apply to the use of illegal drugs today. People use all sorts of drugs to medicate their pain and problems. Whether in an attempt to escape reality or to tap into another level of consciousness, drug abuse is merely an effort to pursue a solution to problems and achieve peace through something other than God himself. If you think about it, that's fundamentally what sorcery supplied for those in Paul's culture—a connection with the supernatural or higher plane of consciousness through a drug-induced state of mind. And it's in this sense that the use of illegal drugs can be comparable to witchcraft. It's worth noting that it's a *spiritual* thing, and thus a spiritual sin. Recreationally using illegal drugs goes way beyond the old "It's bad for your health" or even the "Your body is the temple of the Holy Spirit" argument. There is something inherently spiritual about unlocking the defenses of your mind to entities outside of Christ's influence. Demonically inspired religions and cults are well aware of the mystical and psychic uses of narcotics to cause a person to be open to demon spirits.

Would you delete all the antivirus software off of your computer? Would you use your credit card on an unsecured website? Would you unlock your doors at night during a crime spree in your neighborhood? Would you place your arm into a box filled with venomous snakes, just for the thrill of it?

And why not? Because you're confident that if you did any of the above, eventually someone would take advantage of you—hacking into your accounts, planting viruses, using your credit card, coming into your unlocked home to steal your stuff, or harming you physically. You would eventually get snakebit. Maybe even the first time. And what's true in the physical world is also true in the spiritual world. The difference is that in the spiritual world you know for a fact that you have an enemy who is out to destroy you.[5] This entity is literally trolling the Christian church, looking for an unlocked window or an unprotected mind. So why would a believer voluntarily unlock his or her mind with drugs, knowing that it gives the ultimate evil access to our human hard drives?

If I were to hack into your computer, I certainly wouldn't

want you to know it, would I? I'd much rather stealthily steal information and files from you without you ever knowing I was there. I wouldn't want to crash your computer, but rather would keep it running as long as I needed you. It's a huge misconception about Satan and demons that they're always overt in their influence and activity. The truth is that the vast majority of their time they work covertly, using cleverly devised schemes and strategies to subvert God's work in us.[6] And like a virus or hacker, by the time you recognize their presence, it's usually too late. The damage has already been done. The reality is that for thousands of years demons have used the pathway created by drugs to open a portal into the human mind. Once there, they deposit thoughts that undermine God's truth, weakening a person's defense system against their lies. That may be one of the reasons why God urges us to protect our minds.[7]

A Parade of Zombies

Paul helps us understand that the seed-plant of sin within us affects our social relationships as well, spawning actions involving hatred, discord, jealousy, fits of rage, selfish ambition, dissensions, factions, envy, drunkenness, and orgies. Not the best way to develop a group of friends. Check yourself to see which of these best describes your relationships.

Hatred is an emotion that causes an individual to harbor ill will toward another person. It doesn't mean you seethe with anger. It might mean you trash someone's reputation to someone else.

Discord is created in relationships through conflict and arguing. Different from having a healthy or even heated discussion, this kind of quarreling drives a wedge in friendships and families. It breaks relationships in half for no good reason.

Jealousy can be a good or bad thing, depending on its focus.

Paul told the Corinthians, "I am jealous for you with a godly jealousy."[8] He also told the same people that "love is *not* jealous."[9] So what's the difference? Having a "godly jealousy" means looking out for the best interests of the other person without regard to yourself or personal or selfish motives. It's reflecting the aspect of love that protects. But the jealousy that comes from the zombie inside is all about selfish ambition and envy. It has to do with wanting what someone else has, and it stems from an ungrateful attitude for what God has provided for you.[10]

Fits of rage are emotional reactions manifested when you fail to control your temper. Like a sudden explosion of anger.

Selfish ambition is just what it sounds like: being into something solely for your own glory and benefit. It's all self-centeredness, a "What's in it for me?" attitude.

Dissensions refers to causing divisions in Christian relationships.[11]

Factions is a related term, but it has more to do with dividing believers over opinions related to doctrine, such as pushing your beliefs about minor doctrine to the point at which it divides the body of Christ. (Paul did say that there is a time when it is appropriate to break relationships with those who threaten the integrity of the gospel, but that's wisdom, not factions.[12]) Paul knew all too well that, if left unchecked, factious people would eventually destroy the body of Christ.

Envy is another deadly emotion that comes from the sin nature within. It is a first cousin to jealousy and has a flavor of bitterness to it.

Drunkenness and *orgies* are grouped with the social sins in Paul's letter to the Galatians because they take place, as they did in Paul's day, in the context of friendships and social networks. He was talking about the kind of unrestrained partying that leads to all kinds of sin.

Looking at these sins wears me out. And it also gets a little personal. You may not struggle with outbursts of anger, but may instead be more drawn toward sensuality, impurity, or idolatry. Again, Galatians 5:19–21 wasn't meant to be an exhaustive list of sins produced by the flesh. In case it's not enough for you, Paul was happy to warn us of other deeds produced by our sin nature, among them: nature worship, lesbianism, homosexuality, deceit, gossip, arrogance, the inventing of new kinds of evil, disobedience to parents, a refusal to be loving, the withholding of mercy, unreliability, and applauding those who do wrong.[13] Does all this sound a bit negative to you? Like a "downer"? Or is it simply that pulling up the rug covering the human heart reveals all sorts of unpleasant, crawling creatures?

Truthfully, a lot of people in our generation enjoy the raw horror and gore of the living-dead genre. "Zombie-glam," if you will. I like it too, especially the kind found in books, on TV shows, and in movies. But a film in which a dozen rotting creatures stumble across a lawn toward the front door isn't nearly as scary as what happens in real life. Reality is much more frightening than science fiction. If you really want to encounter evil face-to-face, gaze at these living-dead deeds and tremble. See their rotting, bony fingers reaching out for you. Hear them moan from behind, creeping up on you, eager to sink their diseased incisors into your neck. Smell the stench of their decay in your nostrils. Sense the fear that comes from knowing that these real-life zombies lust for the chance to exploit you and rip a permanent tear in your relationships with God, your family, and your best friends. Maybe you've already witnessed their destructive dominance and display in those relationships. Just know that you and I are fully capable of every one of them, and this is why we have to keep in mind how delicate and susceptible we really are.

Episode Five

FLESH-GHOSTS
AND MONSTERS

Though reliable documentation of zombies' presence in the ancient world is rare, no reputable historian denies their existence. Oral traditions passed down through the ages spoke of such creatures and their grizzly acts, and fortunately, through cave paintings, hieroglyphics, and, later, handwritten scrolls, zombie history has been well documented.

Take the Moabites, for example. Upon conquering the Amaleans in 450 BC, they oversaw the greatest proportionate slaughter of human beings the world has even known. In a three-week campaign, Moabite warriors crossed the Rigaza River in the dead of night and laid siege to the great city of Norcor. Twelve days later, the city gates were breached and every resident destroyed. Death came swiftly and violently. Today, Norcor is nothing more than a large desert mound of rubble and dust.

Following this victory, Moab's King Mizpeth was hailed a world hero. One portion of the Great Tablet, unearthed in 1848 at the Sacred Pyramid of Suzmiz, refers to him as "Mizpeth the Messiah." While clearly hyperbole, it proves there were outbreaks throughout recorded history. You can't get through ninth-grade history without studying the fourteenth-century "Flesh Plague" that swept Europe, when more than 1.5 million perished from a disease that ravaged a large portion of the civilized world. Every person was affected in some way—the peasant as well as the posh—except for a certain segregated religious group who, for reasons unknown, managed to avoid the epidemic in their community. Because of this, rumor spread that *they* were somehow to blame for the zombie scourge. A short-lived persecution ensued.

Then there was the "Rage of 1620," precipitating a mass exodus of pilgrims fleeing England to pursue freedom and safety in the New World. These brave pioneers set out for a new life, free from the threat of terror, to begin a society "devoid of the depraved zombie-devils."[1] One early settlement, New Gloucester, began at a remote spot on what is now the North Carolina coast. In 1622, they landed with 160 persons, who went to work—clearing land, constructing homes, cultivating farms, and breeding animals. A school was constructed and a basic judicial system agreed upon. Even a church was built. The harvests proved plentiful, as food flowed in abundance. New Gloucester had no known enemies and was America's first fully functioning democracy.

Twenty-two months after these first settlers landed on the untouched Atlantic Coast beaches, a delegation from another colonial community (in the area now known as Virginia) paid a visit to New Gloucester. Led by Sir Edward Licant, the famed English physician and former member of Parliament, the twelve-man goodwill ambassador team had come to fact-find and perhaps learn the secrets to New Gloucester's success. However, upon their arrival they found not a single person there. No one *alive*, that is. Eventually they discovered their bodies, or what was left of them—bone and rotting flesh scattered in pieces about the village. All human (or better, *formerly* human) residents lay in the spots where they had died, their bodies divided into sections. As Sir Edward later noted in his diary, "All perished, it seemed, on the selfsame day." Licant further observed, "The skulls of these pioneer villagers were invaded in some fashion. Broken like a potter's jug in several places—their contents emptied."

Continuing their investigation, Licant's team discovered the last "survivor" of this mysterious massacre. The man was later identified as Thomas Cornwall, a farmer and father of two. Cornwall's body was found inside the village church, outside whose barred doors were a dozen corpses, each bearing an ax wound to the head. Inside, slumped over the steps leading to the pulpit, was Cornwall himself, a single shot through the temple. An English dueling pistol lay beside him. He had barricaded himself inside the house of worship after slaying his former friends. It was the final desperate act of a hopeless man.

Again, from Sir Edward's diary:

The mere thought among us that the ghoulish rage we had hoped to leave behind in England had followed us to the new world sent a collective chill up one's spine. To a man, we pledged our minds and fortunes to fight this ancient evil henceforth from that day. Even if death itself be our lot, every farmer among us became a warrior and every statesman a soldier as we readied ourselves for battle, should these shuffling demons appear among our own ranks or, God forbid, even our own families.

The British gentleman was so aghast at the ghoulish discovery, and fearing another outbreak like the great Flesh Plague, he ordered that the bodies at New Gloucester be collected and burned. After locating the settlement's documents and official records, the twelve-man party then set fire to the houses, public buildings, and barns. Word was sent back to England, whereupon King James I decreed, "No settlement shall ever be constructed upon the spot once occupied by New Gloucester." And though he had no legal jurisdiction here, his royal wish was gladly honored. Today, if you drive along the North Carolina coast up Highway 70 near Goose Bay, you'll see a lone, faded sign that reads:

> Near this spot in 1624, the English settlement of
> New Gloucester once stood.

And if you go there, pull over and spend a few minutes gazing across the road into the field beyond. At first, all you'll hear is coastal wind whistling through the tall grass, perhaps a flock of ducks breaking the silence. But close your eyes and imagine what horrible shrieks and moans must have filled the Carolina salt air some four hundred years ago.

This brings up another interesting story—one regarding Heinrich Von Zweig, a German biophysicist based in Berlin in the 1930s. Von Zweig fought for Germany in the First World War. During this time, his infantry unit found itself pinned down by French machine gun and mortar fire for three weeks. Cold, hungry, and exposed to the elements, the soldiers discovered that day and night had become indistinguishable in the fog of war. Red-hot shrapnel scattered like swarms of bees whenever a shell exploded nearby.

Von Zweig was assigned to infantry. His primary duty was running dispatch orders from one muddy trench to another. There were no telecommunication devices available in those days, so men were the messengers. Courier duty was reserved for a special soldier (a lance corporal, or "*Gefrieter*"). As expected, these dispatch unit *Gefrieter*s suffered high casualties.

At twenty, Von Zweig was one such dispatcher. Having been on the front lines for just a week, he and an unknown *Gefrieter* were running their dispatches when a French mortar shell exploded between them. The soldiers were catapulted into the air, landing with great force on the scorched landscape. Von Zweig awoke to discover that he was still alive, though severely wounded in the leg. Through the lingering smoke-haze, he scanned the ground, looking for the other dispatcher and hoping he had survived the awful blast. Locating him, Heinrich crawled though a barrage of machine-gun fire, finally arriving at the man's side. The corporal was unconscious and bleeding, but alive. Von Zweig dragged his fellow soldier some thirty yards to safety, where medics took over.

Having been miraculously spared, Heinrich cared for his comrade, who had suffered a massive concussion. The young corporal, with Von Zweig faithfully by his side, languished for days, lapsing in and out of consciousness. Eventually, the man was transported from the battlefield and taken to a field hospital away from the front lines. After the war, Heinrich spent several days in a German hospital to remove shrapnel from his leg. Following his discharge, he attended the University of Heidelburg and then in 1928 earned his doctorate in biophysics from the University of Berlin's prestigious School of Human Research.

One day, in 1931, Heinrich attended a men's rally at a local Berlin *biergarten*. There, a charismatic speaker captivated the doctor's attention, and Von Zweig recognized him as the soldier whose wounds he had tended all those years ago.

After the gathering, Heinrich introduced himself, and the two men commandeered a corner booth, talking long into the night, reminiscing about their paths since the Great War. The man explained how he had refounded the National Socialist German Workers' Party, and that he was bringing to reality his dreams for a revitalized Germany—dreams born in a war trench years earlier. That man was none other than Adolf Hitler. So full of gratitude for what Von Zweig had done for him years before, the Nazi Party leader pledged his undying loyalty to him right there in that *biergarten* booth.

"I must repay your kindness to me," Hitler promised, whereupon he promptly offered Heinrich a position on the medical research arm of what soon became the dreaded German Third Reich. Eager to advance his career, Von Zweig accepted the offer. From his laboratory in Berlin, Germany's new chief medical researcher developed a specialty in disease and genetic exploration, and quickly rose to the top of his field. It was around this time that a zombie outbreak occurred in Wiesbaden (1936). Hitler immediately dispatched an infantry unit along with several tanks from the Fourth Panzer Division. Once there, most of the living dead were killed on site. However, a few were captured for further study. Hitler ordered for these ghouls to be shackled and transported to Dr. Von Zweig's Berlin laboratory at once. The doctor spent four months studying the beasts before submitting his official report to the Führer, which revealed that they relentlessly pursued human flesh until decapitation or a well-placed shot to the head destroyed them for good (bullets shot elsewhere had no effect).

The Nazi Führer was elated upon receiving this report. He immediately dictated that Von Zweig begin "breeding" (through forced infection) an elite core of Nazi zombie soldiers to unleash upon the enemies of the Fatherland. Heinrich instantly understood the insanity of the idea: such a plan would bring about the death of all Europe, and ultimately Germany itself. His research indicated that zombies could reproduce through attack and infection faster than mankind could destroy them. He communicated this to Hitler in an attempt to dissuade him from his demented idea, but the dictator flatly refused to accept such "feeble excuses!"

Hitler also failed to factor one thing into this equation. His chief medical researcher possessed something the Führer had long since abandoned: a conscience. Von Zweig would not allow himself to be a part of the slaughter of innocents. This was not science. It was genocide, and not what he had signed up for. No matter how great his allegiance to Hitler, he could not do such a thing. So Von Zweig made an unthinkable decision, and a dangerous one no German major dared make.

He disobeyed his Führer.

Realizing this meant execution by firing squad, Dr. Von Zweig escaped under cover of darkness to Hamburg. From there he bribed the captain of a fishing trolley on its way to Grimsby, England. After three months hiding in London, he caught a freighter out of Southampton, eventually disembarking two weeks later in New York City. Immediately flagged by the United States Office of Strategic Services, Dr. Von Zweig was intercepted and "invited" by our own military intelligence community to share what he knew about Hitler. In return for his cooperation, he was allowed to continue his research, provided his first order of business was to discover the cause and source of zombie-ism. As fortune would have it, Von Zweig had smuggled a trunk containing all his notes, along with a sealed glass vial containing a zombie flesh sample.

Meanwhile, back in Berlin, upon discovering that Von Zweig had fled, taking his research with him, Hitler flew into an insane rage. He immediately charged his minion Joseph Goebbels with finding a final solution to dispose of his enemies.

Following several years of study, Von Zweig successfully isolated the virus, thus satisfying his contract with America. His only request was that the discovery bear his name. President Roosevelt agreed, and Zweig-38 was born. However, given the growing climate of distrust toward Hitler at the time, it was decided that a German name wouldn't be appropriate. So it was shortened to "Z-38," and has been known as such ever since. The average person today probably couldn't even tell you what the *Z* stands for.

As for the good doctor? He retired in 1944 at the age of fifty, having been provided a generous retirement pension, courtesy of the United States government. Relocating from Washington, D.C., to the little town of Harbor Lakes, Pennsylvania, Von Zweig settled into a quiet, unobtrusive existence. He never married, filling his days instead writing his memoirs and tending to his garden. He enjoyed long walks, prescribed by his doctor to alleviate the pain in his leg, a lingering reminder of his days in the First World War. Aided by a cane, Heinrich regularly explored the remote, two-lane dirt roads that lined the countryside near his tiny farm. Then, on April 2, 1945, while on one of his walks, he was struck by a hit-and-run driver. His body was discovered several days later when a passerby noticed a broken cane lying in the road.

There was much speculation around this time in the intelligence community that this had been no random accident, but rather a carefully executed assassination plot ordered by Adolf Hitler himself. Ironically, just one month later, while all of Germany collapsed around him, Hitler would take his own life in a Berlin bunker. A secretary assigned to one of the Bunker generals now claims she once heard the aging, senile Hitler shout, "Germany is lost! Where are you, Von Zweig? Where is your gratitude for all I have done for you? I will find and destroy you! I swear it!"

If true, then one of history's worst devils exacted vengeance on the man who refused to give him the ultimate weapon of mass destruction.

That's the rumor anyway.

Chapter 5

THE ULTIMATE
CON ARTIST

I don't trust me.

—Anonymous

What a Heel

Once there were two brothers—twins, actually—born only minutes apart. Fraternal, not identical. The older boy turned out to be the outdoorsy type—loved hunting, weapons, and wild game. He also liked to work the land. At birth this brother was rough and reddish, a foreshadowing of the kind of man he would become. So his nickname became "Red." The younger twin, Jake, was the polar opposite of his older brother. He preferred the comforts of home to the outdoors. While his older brother enjoyed the taste of wild game, Jake's palate was suited for a milder diet. He was more even-tempered, very much unlike his sibling's risk-taking approach to life.

One day Red came home to find Jake in the kitchen, cooking a stew of wild game. It smelled so good, and Red was famished and tired from working outdoors.

"Hey, Jake, let me have some of that stew."

"Forget it. It's mine," his younger twin replied.

"Aw, c'mon, man. I'm starving. Have a heart for your older brother," Red begged.

"Hmm. Let me think. Okay, but on one condition," Jake said.

"Name it. Anything."

"I'll trade you this bowl of delicious stew for your portion of Dad's inheritance," Jake demanded.

A ridiculous offer, of course. However, never under-estimate the desperation of a man with a craving. Red was so incredibly delirious with hunger that he agreed to his brother's proposal.

"Fine. Besides, I'm gonna die anyway unless I get some food inside me. I'll do it. Gimme that stew!"

"First you have to swear," Jake said.

"Okay, okay. I swear. Now, let's have it!"

So that day, Red gave up his inheritance for a bowl of hot grub.

• • •

Fast-forward many years later, and their dad is on his death-bed. Blind, feeble, and hardly able to sit up, he sends for his oldest son to come to his bedroom.

"Son, I'm old and I don't know how much longer I have. Would you be willing to grant a dying man his final wish?"

"Certainly, Father. Anything. Just name it," Red replied.

"I wish I had a dish of my favorite food. Would you go hunting and bring back some wild game and cook it for your old dad before he dies?"

"Of course I will, Dad. Anything for you," Red promised.

So Red grabbed his hunting gear and charged out into the woods.

Meanwhile, his mother had secretly been listening to the whole conversation. This mom had a favorite son, and it wasn't Red. Jake was Momma's boy, and so, knowing that her husband was dying but that he would impart a blessing—intended for Red—before he died, she immediately called Jake and related what was going down.

"Here's what we're going to do. Go and fetch me two baby goats from our flocks, and I'll make your dad his favorite food. Then disguise yourself as your brother and get the blessing before he gets back from hunting."

"But, Mom, what if Dad touches me and realizes I'm not Red? He'll get mad and curse me instead of blessing me."

"If that happens and he does recognize you, I'll take the blame for it. Don't worry."

So Jake did what his mom proposed, dressing up in his brother's old hunting clothes.

Entering his father's bedroom, he greeted him and gave him a hug, prompting the old man to remark, "That's odd. You smell like Red, but you talk like Jake."

To make a long story short, the deception worked. Jake got his father's blessing, and when his brother returned and brought the prepared meal to his dad, they both realized what Jake had done. And from that day forward, Red hated his brother and wanted to kill him.[1] A remarkable story, and a true one. But that's what life was like for Isaac and sons, Jacob and Esau. And while big bro Esau wasn't perfect, Jacob was a straight-up deceiver. A two-faced con artist. With one hand he'd shake yours, while the other would be digging in your pocket.

● ● ●

Now fast-forward about fourteen hundred years to a man named Jeremiah. With his thoughts inspired by God's Spirit, he was trying to think of a word to describe the crooked-ness of the human heart. He finally landed on this one: "The heart is *deceitful* above all things and beyond cure. Who can understand it?"[2] And in doing so, he used the same root word as the Hebrew name Jacob. The ancient Hebrews con-sidered the "heart" to be the center of a person's intellect, conscience, and will. So what Jeremiah was saying is that our intellect, conscience, and will are all deceitful. Corrupt and untrustworthy. Keep in mind, Jeremiah lived in some pretty sad times himself, having earlier written, "Beware of your friends; do not trust your brothers. For every brother is a deceiver, and every friend a slanderer."[3] In other words, every brother is a "Jacob." What a legacy. But consider that for any relationship to work, no matter what kind, there has to be *trust*. Trust is the foundation upon which all friend-ships, romances, partnerships, businesses, and marriages are built. It's the glue that holds them together. If a person can't trust his friend, then he can no longer have a friendship with him. What if your best friend kept stealing money from you? Or what if you told her a secret, and the next thing you know, she posted it as her Facebook status? How would that make you feel? What impact would that have on your relationship? Breaking confidence once or twice can be dealt with, but if someone continues to do it, the friendship will suffer irrepa-rable damage. And you will be sure not to share any more confidential information with that person. I've known people like that. You have to be careful not to divulge too much personal information to them because they just can't keep a secret. Or worse, they somehow use the information against you. They simply aren't reliable. They can't be trusted. We often refer to these kinds of people as "two-faced," "unreli-able," or "fickle."

An Inside Job

It's bad enough to have a friend who would treat you like that. But here's a more shocking truth. There's someone closer to you than a friend who deals in this kind of deceit every day. It's not someone you can just "de-friend" or delete from your phone's address book. It can't simply be ignored either, because it's a part of you. It goes with you wherever you go. Twenty-four hours a day. It's with you at home, school, and work. It drives with you in the car and sits with you when you're at the computer. It goes on dates and hangs out with you when you're with friends. And it's constantly talking to you. Thinking for you. Prompting emotions. Suggesting choices. It's your *heart*. Not that fleshy muscle that pumps your blood, but rather the immaterial part of you. In fact, it's you *yourself*. Here's the deal. As a believer in Christ, you now have two natures—old and new, sinful and spiritual, fleshly and godly—and because the sinful part is still there, you feel drawn away from God.

So how does your own heart deceive you? How does it cheat and scam you? What methods does it use to trick you into sin and rejecting God? We're told to "trust ourselves" and "follow our hearts," but is that really a good idea?

For starters, our deceitful hearts promise pleasure, but it's usually the kind that ultimately delivers pain. It deals in illusions and dreams masquerading as reality and truth. And it gives you just enough pleasure to make you think it's real and lasting. But it soon disappears.[4] It also promises freedom, and everybody wants to be free, right? Personal freedom is considered among the greatest rights we have. But there's a lie embedded in this kind of freedom, and it's found in the misguided advice, "If it makes you happy, do it." We all want to be happy, so how could something be wrong if it makes you feel so happy? This attitude is not the same as having a healthy, independent spirit, or being creative or nonconformist. Those can be really good things in a world that pressures you to be like everyone else. Instead, it's the twisted notion that says true freedom is found through independence from any authority.

This idea is founded on the premise that most authority is either abusive, tyrannical, or incompetent. And no one wants to be ruled under the iron fist of a cruel parent, boss, teacher, dictator, or tyrannical government. The reality is that not all authority is bad and not all freedom is fun. Freedom from parental authority is awesome at the right time, but also carries the responsibilities of paying all your own bills, doing the laundry, and all things associated with adulthood and "freedom."

True freedom also isn't the same as *absolute* freedom (doing literally anything you desire). In the context of a relationship with Christ, absolute freedom (including freedom from God) is not a good thing. That logically leads to chaos and anarchy. Instead, freedom is like someone loaning you his car. Enjoy it, but don't abuse it. All you have to do is look around at those who have allowed themselves to do whatever they wanted to in life. And where does this abuse of freedom ultimately get you? Slavery, and here's why.

When making choices in life, we can falsely assume that those choices take priority over the consequences of those choices. There's freedom to have sex outside of marriage, but there is no freedom in the consequences of a ruined life, or one that is changed through pregnancy and the raising of a child. There's freedom to do drugs, but no freedom in having to support a $1,000-a-week drug habit. There's freedom to steal, but no freedom in jail. It's deception to think that the answer to life is found in the ability to make any decision you want, regardless of what God, society, or others may say. The choice to do whatever pleases our flesh can end up putting us in ultimate bondage, chained in the handcuffs of recurring guilt and shame. Or something worse.

But this deceptive heart desires freedom from all authority. It doesn't like being told what to do. It hates being restricted or held back. It promises peace, contentment, and satisfaction through living without God, but in the end delivers only emptiness. Solomon (a very wise man) listened to his heart and shut God out for a while. He made choices without consulting him. The result was that he followed other gods and settled into a vain, worthless existence.[5] The peace and fulfillment he was looking for eluded him. And he paid dearly for it. And the sin nature in all of us protests, *Yeah, but that wouldn't happen to me.*

The point is that we really can't fully trust our own thoughts, conscience, emotions, or choices. They're broken. Busted. Ruined. Spoiled, like milk or hamburger meat gone bad. And yet carefully disguised as something good and desirable. When we think of cunning and deceit, we often think of a fox or a snake, but according to Scripture, our hearts are deceitful even above these creatures ("above *all* things"). The longer we live, the greater our ability and capacity for sin. And "who can understand it?" Scripture asks. It's a rhetorical question. The answer is, "No one." The depths of the human heart can never be fully explored, but the Bible says that from it flows the "wellspring of life."[6] So if we're going to drink from it, we should make sure it's clean and protected.

Jacob was a master deceiver. And so is the human heart. Perhaps the freedom we're all looking for isn't freedom to do what we want, but rather freedom *from* the con artist inside. And maybe that's why Solomon wrote, "He who trusts in himself is a fool, but he who walks in wisdom is kept safe."[7]

Episode Six

TACTICS OF THE LIVING DEAD

Patricia Forman was cleaning up from breakfast when the intercom buzzer rang in her home.

"Mrs. Forman, your son is here to see you," the voice on the intercom announced.

"Thanks, Bill. Send him through," she responded.

Patricia moved into Farmington Heights exactly one year to the day after her husband's death. John Forman's life insurance was enough to build her new house, and the boys donated a portion of what their father had left them to purchase the land. It was a decision they'd made within twenty-four hours of their dad's funeral.

Farmington Heights is a gated community twenty miles east of Corazon City. Following an outbreak of zombie attacks five years ago in nearby Clifton Springs, Jacob Green, a local developer, purchased sixty acres of land on the side of a gently sloped mountain. Once the land was zoned for a housing development, the lots began to sell. The price tag for a one-acre lot is $75,000. Green's brainchild was to establish a protected "Viable Village." As advertised in his marketing brochures, this semi-self-sustaining compound includes:

- communal lease gardens
- walking trails
- a meditation garden and chapel
- a clubhouse for parties and gatherings
- a swimming pool
- a water treatment facility

In addition, Farmington Heights employs state-of-the-art innovations in security, including:

- A single gate for entering and exiting. This gate is constructed of solid steel, fourteen feet high and more than three inches thick. It's virtually impenetrable and can only be opened from the inside. It takes thirty seconds to fully deploy, and in the unlikely event of a power failure, it has its own dedicated backup generator.
- A fourteen-foot-high perimeter wall.
- Eight guard stations, one at each corner and four equally dispersed between them, all with armed guards, 24/7.
- Video surveillance along the perimeter and inside the grounds, monitored by a command center located in a sealed bunker just inside the gate.

Every "Green Built" house has access to Farmington's security cameras via a password-protected website. The houses' ground-floor walls are virtually impenetrable, with no doors or windows on that level. The second floor is accessible only by a uniquely designed motorized staircase, which can be raised or lowered in about fifteen seconds. These stairs lead to a wooden deck, and from there the house's main level is accessed. Each home has three bedrooms, two bathrooms, a kitchen, a living room area, and a large room downstairs. This ground level has a sizable storage room, perfect for outbreak scenarios. There's also a built-in air-filtration system and a generator on the ground floor. Residents are encouraged to purchase food and supplies sufficient for a two-month lockdown in the unlikely event of a zombie siege.

There are three slit-like "windows" in the ground floor, whose walls are constructed entirely of cement block. These uniquely shaped slits are just big enough to give the homeowner a peek at what's going on outside, or more important, a space through which to maneuver the barrel of a rifle or shotgun.

There's only one interior stairway leading to the ground-floor level, ensuring quick access to safety should a retreat be necessary. The door at the bottom of this stairway incorporates huge deadbolt locks. These steel bars are secured from the inside, preventing any penetration from the upper floor and making the ground-floor bunker virtually "zombie-proof."

Total cost for this protective "peace of mind"? Around $425,000 (including the cost of the lot), plus a $400 monthly security charge.

From the start, critics labeled the development "Green's Getaway" and "Cowards' Compound," with a local columnist writing an op-ed piece declaring it "a retreat for the rich who are too sorry and cowardly to live with the rest of us." Green counterattacked with a hastily called press conference, claiming that once the inevitable next outbreak hits, "We'll see who's sorry. We'll be safe inside our homes, watching TV, while you're running for your life or getting your brains devoured by a zombie!" End of press conference.

Lot sales dramatically increased the following day.

And now there's talk of a sister community like Green's to be built south of the city sometime in the next year.

• • •

Patricia lowered the motorized staircase from the inside.

"Hi there, honey," she said, greeting her son. Crystal was with him. "What brings you way out here? Everything okay?"

"Does a son need an excuse to see his momma?" Ben responded.

"Of course not. But when a momma hasn't seen her son in several weeks, it makes her wonder. It's a sixth sense God gives mothers, and it's rarely wrong."

Ben gave his mom a long hug. Patricia gave Crystal a warm smile.

"You kids come on in. I'll fix some breakfast."

Patricia flipped a switch, and the staircase locked in place.

Once inside, Ben and Crystal sat on the living room couch.

"Mom, I'm really not hungry. I had pancakes last night at the Breakfast Shack," Ben explained.

"*That* place?" Patricia shot back. "Why, they don't know the first thing about pancakes. First off, think about who's working there—"

"Mom," Ben interrupted. "Calm down. I've already given Crystal the 'My mom makes the best pancakes in the world' speech. Okay?"

"Well, all right. But I worry about you sometimes. You look too thin. Are you eating? Are they paying you enough at that surfboard company?"

"Mom, yes. I'm fine. I make enough money. And it's a skateboarding magazine," said Ben, laughing. "Just some hot tea would be nice for now."

"Hot tea it is," Patricia said, heading into the kitchen.

Ben got up and strolled around his mom's living room, looking at the dozens of pictures she had used to decorate her home. A flood of memories came leaping out of those photographs. Walking over to the mantel, Ben picked up a framed family picture, taken in Arizona.

"Crystal, look at this," he said, motioning with his hand. "Okay, the story here is, summer before I left for college, Dad had this idea we'd go to the Grand Canyon, sleep in tents, and be 'Wilderness Family' for a week. But Mom vetoed that, saying she wouldn't go unless we stayed in a nice lodge. I'll give you one guess where we stayed. The whole time Dan and I kept scaring Mom by pretending to jump off the edge."

Ben turned the frame over and recognized his mother's handwriting:

> Last family vacation together. Summer '04. Ben away at college. Dan off to Basic Training.

He carefully placed the framed photograph back on the mantel.

"Hot tea ready!" Patricia announced. "Sorry. All I had was mint-flavored."

"Perfect, Mom," Ben assured her.

"So, to what do I owe the privilege of seeing you two this morning?" Patricia asked.

"Well . . ." Ben paused, glancing over at Crystal. "Something happened last night. Something . . . bad."

Patricia furrowed her brow.

"Don't worry, Mom. It's not about us," he said, quickly looking at his girlfriend again. "It's about . . . *them*."

Them.

That's all Ben really had to say. He knew his mom understood what he was talking about. People generally speak of zombies in such ways, giving the creatures a variety of names—the *things*, the *living dead*, or *flesh-devils*. In the Forman family, *them* was all you needed to say when describing these former humans. Mention that word to Patricia Forman, and the Southern woman's usually pleasant demeanor turned to a simmering cauldron of bitterness.

"I know the topic upsets you, Mom. But I wanted to tell you before you read it in the paper or saw it on the news." But Ben also wanted his mom to know so she wouldn't worry about him, as she often did. He told what had happened to him the previous night.

Listening to her son relate his experience, Patricia was reminded why she had moved to Farmington Heights. She was grateful she didn't have to worry about things like that, especially after the tragic incident at her previous home.

The three of them talked for another hour, mainly about Ben's work. Then Ben kissed his mom and promised that he and Crystal would come for dinner the following week.

● ● ●

Driving through the huge gate guarding Farmington Heights, Crystal reached over and gently stroked Ben's hand.

"So . . . what now, handsome?" she said.

Ben looked at her and thought about what a comfort she'd been since the incident, not so much as a girlfriend, but more as a true friend.

"Hey, thanks for riding out here with me. And thanks again for being there last night. It means a lot."

"You know I'm there for you. And I always will be, okay?" she said, leaning over and kissing him on the cheek. "But you haven't answered my question yet. What are you going to do now?"

"My boss let me take a couple of days off, just to get my head together. I may give Dan a call and see if he has any free time this weekend. I haven't seen him in a while, and I'd like to drive down and see if he can shed some light on all this. I don't know. I just have a bad feeling inside."

● ● ●

After his dad's death, Dan Forman had returned to Fort Bragg and resumed army life, but his soldier buddies could tell he wasn't the same man. Edgy and easily angered, he spent his free time alone, mostly reading while the other guys were playing cards, working out, or hanging at the officers' club. After serving his country stateside without being deployed, Dan was feeling useless, as if his talent was being wasted. He was tired of exercise drills and combat simulations. He was ready to do what he was trained for. He wanted off the sidelines and in the *game*.

About this time a buddy suggested he check out the ZTF Training Academy. Knowing his four-year commitment to the Army would end soon, Dan applied for and was accepted into the elite Zombie Task Force Academy Training Program. This course, a sixteen-week combat-training regimen based deep in the mountains of North Georgia, rivaled any Special Forces unit the military offered, combining the resources of the FBI, CIA, and the United States military. From their home base near the Georgia-Tennessee border, ZTF units can deploy to any spot in the country within a few hours. These highly trained teams are only called in for crises, as local police and ZTF-sanctioned law enforcement usually take charge of smaller-scale skirmishes (like when Dan's dad was attacked).

The ZTF application process weeds out more than two-thirds of its applicants. To begin with, candidates must have a minimum four years prior military service. Then there's a rigorous physical aptitude test, and a written exam regarding the philosophy and strategy of the ZTF. There's also an extensive medical and psychological evaluation. If you pass all of the above, you earn the privilege of appearing before a review board that verbally grills you for a few hours. A thumbs-up here gets you conditionally accepted into the Academy, officially beginning the sixteen-week program. "Camp Hell" begins with a recruitment class of 120 guys, with fewer than half making the final cut.

ZTF instructors relentlessly hammer their new recruits, throwing every conceivable challenge at them. Day 1—crawl on your stomach a quarter mile through mud, slime, and an assortment of dead animal parts in various stages of decomposition, all while live ordnances explode nearby. Days 2 through 12 begin at 5 a.m. with twelve-mile ruck marches, followed by more physical training and classroom instruction. The next fourteen weeks are filled with obstacle courses, hand-to-hand combat, team-building exercises, rifle-range and marksmanship training, orienteering and land navigation, search-and-rescue training, certification in air assault from helicopters, and transport parachute jumps. And most of this takes place on about two to three hours of sleep per night. There are containment strategies to study and master, and battlefield medical certifications to achieve—to the end that every ZTF soldier is a one-man fighting machine, though he never fights alone. No soldier goes anywhere on a mission by himself. Ever. Not in *this* war. Get separated from your squad, have a weapon jam, become trapped inside a host of zombies while low on ammo—and you're dead meat. Literally. It's the cardinal rule of ZTF warfare: no man alone. You can't win with one. "Lose your buddy, lose your life." ZTF operates in squads of twelve men, with each man assigned to a "battle buddy." They fight side by side at all times and are together from the moment they leave base until their boots hit asphalt upon completion of the mission. No exceptions.

But perhaps the most difficult portion of this training involves protocol in the event a fellow soldier is bitten or infected during a mission. ZTF soldiers know that if this occurs, it is their sworn duty to protect their squad and their country by terminating the infected man on the spot. It's something no soldier likes to think about, but it's the reality of the current conflict. Nobody wants to have to take out the man next to you—the guy who just minutes before could have saved your life—but if the situation presents itself, duty *demands* that you pull that trigger, or in a matter of minutes, you'll be next. It's the kind of reality that brings home the seriousness of zombie warfare, and what's at stake.

Dan Forman was pushed to the limit at ZTF training, almost to the breaking point. That's why so few make it all the way from "Camp Hell" to graduation.

Some don't even last twenty-four hours.

"Honestly?" Dan later confessed to a friend. "Don't tell my old drill sergeant, but those sixteen weeks at Camp Hell made army boot camp seem like being on a kiddie ride at Disneyland." He quickly added, "Not that I've ever done that."

Graduation day was the proudest moment of Dan's life. And when his commanding officer pinned that coveted ZTF logo patch on his sleeve, Dan dutifully saluted and said, "Thank you, sir."

But privately, deep down inside, in that place where the fire in a man's heart burns, Dan whispered, *This one's for you, Dad.*

Chapter 6

DESCENT

All through the night, I me mine, I me mine, I me mine.
—George Harrison

The Abyss

Okay, now it's time to do some *honesty*. The brutal kind. There's a lot of talk about "authenticity" these days among some churches and Christ-seekers. It's become one of those buzzwords that Christians have adopted. Sometimes we act as if we invented it or something. It seems to go very well with lattes and soul patches. Anyway, once you get beyond the coolness of the word, then comes the hard work of actually *becoming* authentic. Apparently this authenticity thing is not something we get at birth, although, like the birth experience, authenticity can be traumatic. It also involves being naked. With this kind of realness, people begin to see you for who you really are. They get a peek at things you'd rather they not see. And like being naked, it's uncomfortable and embarrassing (not to mention frowned upon in public). That's because you're basically afraid that if people saw the real you, they might reject you. So you decide to remain fully clothed, covering up your imperfections. That way we can all continue playing the game many church people play—you know, the "I'm fine. You're okay. Life is great, and so is God" game?

But we're not as fine as we think we are. And since we're not playing games here, let's take things a bit deeper, shall we? To the next level. Let's go beyond being *somewhat* authentic and try being totally honest with ourselves. I'd like you to take an imaginary rope and tie it off at the surface, then begin a slow rappel down into that deep, dark abyss of your heart. All the way down to the place where "it" lives. The beast. The monster. The creature. That "thing" inside that you hate. Your inner zombie.

Once your feet have finally touched the chasm floor, you look back up to notice a faint light shining from above, but it's not enough to help you see much down here. You spot an old torch mounted on the cave wall. Removing it from its perch, you light it. Things once hidden are now revealed in the flickering torchlight. Bones, trash, and filth are scattered all around, along with empty poison bottles, pornography, bloody knives, bitter roots, dirty rags, rotten fruit, and feces. A sickening, foul odor fills the subterranean den. The walls ooze a sticky substance, contributing to the vile stench.

You feel dirty just being here.

Then, when you thought it couldn't get any worse, you hear movement coming from a black hole in the cavern wall. Directing your torch toward the sound, you're not prepared for what your squinting eyes see. Slithering out of that hole is a creature more disgusting and repulsive than anything you've ever beheld. No computer-generated Hollywood monster has come close to portraying the wickedness of this demon. The skin of this malevolent mutant is dry, rough, cracked, and seeping with disease. Its eyes are sunk into its sockets, as black as coal. They have adapted to the dimly lit dungeon environment. This beast has teeth accustomed to tearing flesh. A half-decayed tongue protrudes out of its mouth, licking its cracked lips slowly back and forth, lusting for the next taste of flesh. Raising its rotting nose into the air, it picks up your scent.

There's an old, dingy mirror hanging crookedly on the cavern wall so the creature can admire itself. Though its face is horrendous and revolting, it can't see and thus invents an image of its own imagination. What's left is a perverted, dim reflection of what once was beauty. You lift your torch, which is rapidly burning out, and turn to look into that mirror. You widen your eyes as a paralyzing jolt of terror sends a sudden shockwave through your body. The reflection in the mirror is that of the monster! And now you know the identity of the one who lives in this dark abyss. The hellish zombie creature of the cavern is *you*!

That's authenticity.

Disturbing, yes? But before you panic and frantically climb out of the hole, contemplate this: your descent into this cavern is comparable to taking God's witness stand and confessing to him that you're guilty. The "whodunit" mystery of your entire life is that "*YOU*dunit"! You're the criminal. The thief. The murderer. The cheat. The scoundrel. And that's bad news.

And just before starting your ascent, come to grips with the implications of this gory yet glorious self-revelation. Agree with the truth. *Own* it, and own up to it. *Believe* it. And the moment you do, something strange happens. Something within *you*. Nothing changes about the beast down there. It continues to decay and smell. But something else happens. Something originating from above, where the light is. That dim ray from up top suddenly becomes brighter. Your torch below finally burns out. You don't need it anymore. You can see clearly now. Though you're still present in the pit, you feel an odd sense of relief and release. It's the freedom that only truth can give.[1] Your eyes are opened, perhaps for the first time. And in a different way. You've never seen yourself in such a light. Never quite had this perspective before. Sure, you've admitted many times you were a "sinner." But you never understood the *depth* of your decadence.

You say to yourself, "I see it now. It's all been about *me*. My family is all about *my* happiness and comfort. My friends exist to make *me* feel good about myself. My job is all about *my* success. My college degree is all about *my* prestige. My church is all about what *I* can get out of it. My relationships ultimately revolve around *my* enjoyment. I am the center of my own universe. Everything I do relates back to 'How does it benefit *me*?' Ultimately, nothing else matters. It's *I, me,* and *mine*."

Rewriting Your Testimony

Sounds pretty sad, doesn't it? It almost sounds as bad as what Scripture says about us, that we are *desperately* wicked, deceitful, corrupted, and unable to please God in our natural, sinful condition. Again, this doesn't mean we always act out all our evil thoughts and desires. But it does mean we're unaware that even our noblest deeds are often secretly inspired by a desire to preserve and please self. That's the kind of honesty you can only find on the floor of the abyss.

But society has groomed us to *get*, not give, hasn't it? We've been trained to consume, not contribute. Our materialistic culture can easily turn a Christ-follower into a self-absorbed worshipper. All our blessings and prosperity can easily become a curse if not managed well. As a result of our good fortune, we may subconsciously assume we are entitled to certain things. As if somehow our parents, the government, God, the church, and life actually *owe* us something. But the other side of the coin is that it's also in us from birth. Even before. We are addicted to self. And the craving to please ourselves at all times seems insatiable. It *is* insatiable. We're always hungry for more. All the time.

And why not? It is all about us, right?

Of course, this craving isn't tattooed across our foreheads for everyone to see. It's more like an underground stream eventually finding places to surface in our lives. Self-centeredness. Self-gratification. Self-adoration. A vain preoccupation with appearance. An obsession with self and our image.

Another way our sin nature is dangerous is that it tempts us to use people. To make them our servants, existing only for the purpose of contributing to our happiness. As a result, we like certain people because they make us look good. We like how we feel when we are with them. But is that so wrong? Is it really so bad to enjoy someone's friendship? Of course not. But there is a fine line between "I'm really glad you're my friend. I like being with you" and "You do something for my ego and image."

Until you look in that dungeon soul mirror and see the grotesque image staring back, you will never really understand what Jesus did for you. You might want to go back and reread that last sentence again. To rappel down to that pit of your heart is the best field trip you could ever take. It's where you truly come face-to-face with your sin-self. But the good news is that it's also where you find your desperate need for a Savior. You ever wonder why those who have bottomed out in life seem to have a greater appreciation of their salvation? There is a subculture of celebrity Christians who have *sin*-sational testimonies. Everything from former Mafia hit men, drug dealers, prostitutes, ex-cons, washed-out athletes, actors, etc. And the average Christian thinks, *Wow, do I have a boring testimony, or what? Raised in a Christian home. Believed in Jesus as a child. Never took drugs, slept around, or robbed a bank. Borrr-ing!*

Not so.

The reality is that you actually have the same testimony as those with the spectacular stories. It's just that they may have a better understanding of what it's like when that inner zombie takes complete control of their lives. They may have been more "in touch" with their sin. They wore it. Bathed in it. Slept in it. Breathed it. And everyone could see it. They were aware of how sin-filled they really were before Christ because it was obvious. So when they came to him, they were aware of how deep the pit was and how far up God had lifted them.

Once there was a woman—a prostitute—who heard that Jesus was having dinner at the house of a Pharisee named Simon. She really wanted to see Jesus. So, having already tarnished and destroyed her reputation, she had nothing left to lose and therefore crashed the party. Falling at Jesus' feet, she wept and anointed them with perfume. Her presence there greatly upset the religious leaders, which prompted the Lord to tell them this story.

> "Two men owed money to a certain moneylender. One owed him five hundred denarii, and the other fifty. Neither of them had the money to pay him back, so he canceled the debts of both. Now which of them will love him more?"
>
> Simon replied, "I suppose the one who had the bigger debt canceled."
>
> "You have judged correctly," Jesus said.
>
> Then he turned toward the woman and said to Simon, "Do you see this woman? I came into your house. You did not give me any water for my feet, but she wet my feet with her tears and wiped them with her hair. You did not give me a kiss, but this woman, from the time I entered, has not stopped kissing my feet. You did not put oil on my head, but she has poured perfume on my feet. Therefore, I tell you,

her many sins have been forgiven—for she loved much. But
he who has been forgiven little loves little."

Then Jesus said to her, "Your sins are forgiven."[2]

If we believe that our crime against God is simply "being
imperfect," then our devotion and love for Jesus will be small.
But if we are truly aware of how dark and desperate we really
are, our love for him will be great.

You and that prostitute are not that different.

But thankfully, you don't have to try out all the sins on the
world's buffet in order to really experience God's grace.[3] We
just need to be convinced that we are just as unrighteous as
the people who have participated in those sins.

Strangely, though, it's not always our "badness" that keeps
us from coming to Christ. Sometimes it's our goodness, our
religiosity or "righteousness" blinding us to our true condition.
If we could peel back that thin layer of self-deception that often
covers us, we might understand just how far we are from God.

Jesus Christ beautifully blends selfless humility and obedience. And the light of his character illumines the shaft leading
down into that heart-pit. This light, beaming from his Word,
goes beyond merely exposing the dark places of our soul. It also
X-rays us, revealing the cancer, the broken bone, the blockage.[4]
And why? So we can know just how badly we need the healing
touch of the One who is called the Great Physician. To slay the
zombie we first have to face it.

That's authenticity.

Episode Seven

THE INSATIABLE
CRAVING

After several attempts, Ben eventually reached his brother and arranged a meeting on Saturday. It was a three-hour trip, and he arrived just before noon at the town of Long Creek, just outside ZTF headquarters. Long Creek isn't much more than a wide place in the road, but it does have a few restaurants. Dan suggested they meet at Burrito Loco, the local Mexican eatery.

Ben walked up the wooden steps and into the restaurant. Dan was sitting at a booth, dressed in military fatigues.

"What's up, man?!" he said, standing to greet his brother. "Boy, it's good to see you! You look great!"

"You're not too shabby yourself," Ben replied. "Hey, what's this shiny thing on your chest? You somebody important now?"

"Nah, they slap this on you when you're dumb enough to jump out of a perfectly good airplane," he said, laughing.

Though time and distance separated them, the two brothers remained close. Seeing Dan in that uniform, Ben thought he was one tough-looking hombre.

"Well, let's not stand here gawking at each other all day. I'm starving!" Dan said.

"Me too," Ben agreed.

They had just sat down and begun catching up over chips and salsa when Ben received a text message.

> Just a reminder: don't forget about
> Monday night.

"That your girlfriend? Or just *one* of them?" Dan joked.

"Ha-ha, very funny. Actually, it is a girl, but not my girlfriend. Just someone from work."

"Uh-huh. I bet you've got 'em lining up around the block. My little brother, the ladies' man of Corazon City."

Ben just shook his head while typing his response. No sooner had he finished than another text appeared, this one from Crystal.

> Don't forget about our Monday night
> plans, OK?

"Ugh," he groaned.

"Problem?" Dan inquired.

"Nah. Just something I need to work out." Texting back,

> Got it. I haven't forgotten.

Ben put his phone on silent and slid it to the side.

After giving Dan an update on their mother, he turned the conversation to more serious matters. "Okay," he exhaled, "so this past Wednesday I was working late—"

"How's that going, by the way?" Dan interrupted. "They taking care of you at that place? Paying you pretty good?"

"First off," Ben explained, "the job's going great, and they pay me okay. And second, you sound just like Mom, so quit worrying about me. If I need money, I know who to ask, 'cause you're making the big bucks now, right?"

"Right." Dan chuckled.

"So, anyway, Wednesday night I was walking to my car and stumbled on . . . well, kinda found this dead guy. And he was, like, all . . . you know. Mutilated."

"A zombie attack," interjected Dan.

"Well, yeah," Ben admitted. "A pretty bad one too."

"Most of them are. We got the alert on base Wednesday night about eleven. They put us on standby whenever there's a single episode, just in case it turns into something bigger. But Wednesday's was no big deal. So that was *you*, huh?"

"Yeah, that was me. And yes, it *was* a big deal. Are you kidding? I'm not used to seeing stuff like that, remember?"

"I know. We kinda get a little numb to it after a while," Dan admitted.

The two brothers ordered their food and talked between burritos about various other topics. Ben finished his last bite, and then returned to the subject of the living dead.

"Okay, so there's something I still don't get. Everybody knows it's the virus that causes people to freak out and go zombie, but what I don't understand is what makes them *kill*."

Dan took a long sip of his drink, leaning back.

"That, my friend, is the big question. And one your government is spending about $54 billion in research this year to find an answer. Maybe if we figure that one out, they'll give *us* that money. I'd take it," he said, grinning.

"I'd settle for half that in cash," Ben replied.

Dan continued. "Seriously, I'll tell you what I know, which isn't that much."

"Well, I'm all ears, and I've got all day."

The young soldier hesitated, glancing out the window while thinking about where to begin. "Okay," he said, finally, "what they taught us was that the virus interacts with the central nervous system. But there's still so much we don't understand. It's like studying the universe. We know planets and stuff are out there. And yet we can't fully understand them because we can't get to them. So we're left to *infer* things about them based on what we *can* see. This stuff is way beyond my pay grade, but a buddy of mine put it this way: Let's say you saw footprints on the beach. You'd logically conclude that a person had recently been there, right? So it's like we can't see the virus, but what we do see is its *footprint*, if that makes sense. So based on what we see, we make educated guesses."

"Guesses?" Ben repeated. "You're saying the fate of humanity comes down to *geeks* playing a guessing game?"

"Well . . . yeah!" Dan snapped back. "I mean, come on. The geeks have always come through for us. Geeks got us to the moon, discovered the polio vaccine, brought World War II to an end, and developed your high-tech phone right there. Shoot, most of our tactical gear is invented by guys in lab coats locked away in some basement in the Virginia mountains. Trust me, bro. We *need* the geeks!"

"I know we need the geeks," Ben shot back. "You forget, I'm half-geek myself!" He laughed.

"But see, that's the nature of it, Ben. They have to speculate based on the data they have."

"That's what I'm saying. What data do they have? What do we really *know*?"

"Here's the deal: the Z-virus affects the brain and spinal cord. Most everything in your body is controlled from there, and certain parts of your brain control your impulses. When Z-38 multiplies, it networks with that part of the brain, sending involuntary impulse signals to the body. Thing is, a normal person doesn't always act on their impulses. Let's say you're at a fast-food restaurant and some guy breaks in line ahead of you. You think, *Hey, jerk! You broke in line!* And then you have this random thought about slamming your fist into his *cabeza*. And why don't you follow through? Because you don't want to get arrested, that's why! It's like there's these little 'guard doors' in our minds, keeping us from doing stupid stuff and ruining our lives. But the virus blows those guard doors off their hinges, surging right into the brain spot that controls our worst impulses and urges. And so the infected start acting on their darkest desires and appetites."

"Okay," Ben remarked. "But you still haven't answered me. Why does it make them *kill* and *eat brains*? It's like they actually *enjoy* feasting on flesh."

"You're more right than you know," Dan said, raising an eyebrow.

"What do you mean?" Ben responded, a quizzical look on his face.

"You remember when we were kids, Dad would take us down to the Dairy Bar and buy us ice cream? Remember that old place? I always got a chocolate nut sundae, and you always got—"

"A banana split! Every time," Ben blurted.

"Right. You had this weird obsession with banana splits. I think Mom wanted to get you tested to see if you had some kind of potassium deficiency or something. You'd jump up and down, waiting for the guy to make it for you. You were a weird kid."

"Yeah, whatever. So, what's your point?" Ben said.

"Okay, so think about the *craving* you felt while waiting for that banana split."

"Yeah?"

"Now recall the satisfaction at that first bite. There's another part of the brain that primarily relates and responds to *pleasure*. It produces a sense of euphoria when a person experiences certain things—like eating, playing sports, running, music, or sex. Like what people feel when they fall in love. A hyperelation of the senses. An almost ecstatic experience. And for the infected, *killing* gives them that feeling. I know; hard to believe, right? But with stage 3 and reanimated corpses, the virus kicks into overdrive.

"So, combine uncontrollable, impulsive desire with unimaginable pleasure, and that's how you get zombies."

Ben sat silently while his brother popped an ice cube into his mouth. He still wasn't satisfied and wondered if he was missing something. Dan got up and went to the restroom. When he returned, Ben had their drinks refilled and was ready for round two.

"All right, I get the technical side of what you're saying. I'm tracking with the biology and how chemicals affect people. I knew guys in college who became different people under the influence of alcohol. But I'm not sure I buy the idea that the virus alone is to blame. I'm not saying you're wrong. I'm just saying I'm not totally convinced."

"Well, I don't pretend to know it all, Ben. I'm just telling you what they told us. Of course, some guys on base believe there's also a spiritual side to zombie-ism."

"You're not talking about the 'Old Way' folks, are you?"

"Yes. Look, Mom and Dad never crammed religion down our throats. But they did teach us right from wrong. I've had my share of questions about God-stuff. Like, why'd he even let this virus thing happen? I mean, I do believe in God, and I know zombies are truly evil. And if there's evil, then there has to be *good* as well, right? So I know he's there. You've heard the saying 'There are no atheists in foxholes'? Well, I can tell you from experience there aren't many atheists onboard a Chinook helicopter hovering a hundred feet above downtown Detroit at 3 a.m. either. We're fully protected from head to toe, locked, loaded, and ready to rock, but you should see those guys: bowing their heads, crossing their chests, saying prayers, looking at pictures of girlfriends. I'll bet there's more prayer going on per capita on those helicopters than in any church in America on Sunday morning!"

"Hmmm," Ben mumbled.

"But seriously, a lot of guys in my company see more than just the physical side of this war. They have a way of making sense of it all. They got problems like everybody else, but for some reason they're able to . . . to cope."

"There's this girl I know like that," Ben said. "Same thing. Lost her whole family in a car wreck a few years back. You'd think she'd be strung out on something, medicating the pain at bars every night. But no. She's the most peaceful, positive person I know. Anyway, keep going."

"Yeah, so we come in after a typical mission, and most guys are up half the night, still pumped with adrenaline or drinking. But not these guys. The 'God Squad,' we call 'em—they're in their bunks, sleeping like babies. Like nothing happened. It's like they're immune to the aftershock."

"Aftershock?" Ben asked.

"It's a term we use. Way back when ZTF began, they were still developing mission strategies and tactical maneuvers. As a result, a lot of men got killed. Some were bitten and infected, while others took friendly fire. It's not that zombies are smart. They're actually dumb as dirt. But their impulse strength and tenacity are almost supernatural. They have amazing powers to find their prey. They crave brains so bad they'll go for weeks, even months, pursuing flesh. And eventually they find a way in. Those things are unstoppable, Ben.

"Anyway, these guys would come back from a mission,

and later wake up in a cold sweat, haunted by horrible nightmares: sick, shivering, screaming, throwing up. They've found guys curled up in the fetal position, crying. Many got medical discharges. So 'aftershock' is the second wave of the zombie attack. It's the part of the battle you're not fully prepared for. It doesn't happen on the battlefield. It happens right *here*," Dan said, pointing to his head.

"Have you experienced that?" Ben asked his brother.

"Are you kidding? Every time I set foot back on base, it starts. It's unavoidable . . . just a part of the job."

"So, how do *you* deal with it?"

"Well, you just gotta know it's coming, man. Be prepared," Dan said, with mock arrogance. Then his speech became more serious.

"But no matter how many missions, you're never fully prepared for what you see out there. Sometimes you're taking 'em out in groups, like a real-life video game. And then other times you look into the face of one of those things, and you remember that it was once human. Somebody's mom or dad. Or girlfriend. And then other times . . ." A twinge of guilt colored Dan's voice. "Those times you hesitate before pulling the trigger. That's usually the mistake that gets you killed. But then you're jolted back to reality by that putrid odor of those nasty creatures. Gosh, you never get used to the smell! Guys throw up almost every time just from the odor. I don't know, Ben. There seems to be something deep down inside us telling us mankind was meant for something better. That this zombie thing wasn't in the original blueprint, you know? And even though it's necessary, there's still something unnatural about what we soldiers have to do just to keep the rest of you guys alive. I wonder . . ."

Dan looked intently at the empty glass, as if by staring into it he would somehow find an answer to his dilemma. Then it was like he woke from a daydream.

"But to answer your question. When I get back from a mission, I take a long, hot shower. And when I'm done, I feel clean. Clean on the outside and clean on the inside. I did my job. I performed my duty. I served my country and protected my fellow man. And that makes me feel pretty good right *here*." He pointed to his heart. "Hey, we're not philosophers around here, Ben. We're soldiers. The government's executioners. Glorified garbage men. Warriors. We hunt the hunters. We do the dirty work no one else can do."

"I'm really glad there are people like you, Dan," Ben confessed. "God knows I could never do it."

It was now late afternoon. Dan glanced at his watch.

"Oops. I hate it, but I gotta jet, Benjamin. If I'm not back by 1700, my CO will totally jump down my throat." Dan tossed a twenty on the table, slid out of the booth, and started toward the door. Ben followed him.

"I'm glad we could meet, Dan. It's been too long, and I enjoyed catching up and learning more about what you do. Seriously, it's fascinating."

"Thanks. But we didn't get to *you* and what's going on with *your* job."

"No worries. Next time, okay?"

"Yeah," Dan said with a hint of regret, "next time."

The two men walked outside. Dan carefully positioned the black beret on his head. The prominent red-, green-, and gold-stitched ZTF insignia portrayed a skull smoking a cigar, bordered by a phrase in Latin: "NEX UT TOTUS MORTUUS."[1]

The temperature was dropping in the North Georgia mountains, causing Ben to shiver in his thin, black T-shirt.

"I'm gonna have a few days off for Thanksgiving. I'll see you then, okay?" Dan said, climbing into his truck.

"Oh, for sure. You can meet Crystal, and I know Mom's dying to see you."

Dan waved as he spun out of the parking lot, sending gravel and dirt flying. Ben watched him drive down the mountain road and disappear around a bend. Though the boys had come from the same family, they were as different as daylight and dark. And even though they didn't see each other that much, they remained close, enjoying an uncommon bond.

And that made Ben smile.

• • •

During the three-hour drive back to Corazon City, Ben didn't think once about what had happened on Wednesday. The topic of *them* never entered his mind. Instead, he spent the entire time reminiscing about how great his childhood had been.

And how lucky he was to have a brother like Dan.

Chapter 7

THE SOCIAL NETWORK

Evil brings men together.

—Aristotle

Setting Your Stance

Influence is like a river. And like any river, the more tributaries that feed into it, the stronger it gets. Swimming upstream against that flow is very difficult. But that's exactly what we've been called to do as Jesus' disciples. Paul wrote to the Corinthians, who were surrounded and grossly outnumbered by pagans in a culture very unfriendly to Christians, "Do not be misled: 'Bad company corrupts good character.'"[1] But why would he have to write something like that to people who had already declared their allegiance to Jesus? A couple of reasons: Consider that every single one of those believers was once deeply influenced by the pagan culture in which he or she lived. In fact, the Corinthian church was made up of former idol-worshippers, adulterers, passive and active participants in homosexuality, thieves, drunkards, slanderers, and swindlers.[2]

It's naive to think that people with pasts like this would instantly and magically drop all those habits and lifestyles. That happens, but not always, and typically it takes time. Even then, certain temptations—especially in areas of sexuality and addiction—can haunt people for a lifetime. These believers had been cleansed and made holy in God's sight through faith in Jesus Christ. Yet they still had to be reminded of the powerful influence of unhealthy, toxic relationships.

The second reason Paul told them this was that they were still living in this same pagan culture. They worked and lived with the people in it, many of them close friends who still practiced the aforementioned sins. To think that one Christian can be outnumbered by many ungodly friends and never be affected or influenced in some way is to be deceived.

When Paul wrote this, he was actually quoting verbatim the Greek poet Menander. The Corinthians would have been familiar with this poet. It would be like someone quoting Dylan, Bono, or Coldplay. The point is that truth is truth, no matter who says it.

Solomon wrote something similar in Proverbs 13:20: "He who walks with the wise becomes wise, but a companion of fools suffers harm." He expanded on this idea in Proverbs 2:12–15, writing to his son, "Wisdom will save you from the ways of wicked men, from men whose words are perverse, who leave the straight paths to walk in dark ways, who delight in doing wrong and rejoice in the perverseness of evil, whose paths are crooked and who are devious in their ways."

Again, truth. And again, over time we begin to resemble those with whom we share the most time and the closest relationships.

People who don't have the Holy Spirit living inside them are left to whatever their consciences or some random self-imposed moral or religious code dictate for them. Think about it. You're probably not going to be influenced by that seedy character loitering outside the mall, offering "free candy," or the strange telemarketer offering you the "deal of a lifetime" in prime Florida swampland. Negative. Young or old, it's *friendships* that most influence us. We easily end up becoming an echo of their character. That can be a good thing. Or, you could end up being carried along by the wrong river.

Friendships are the power of association to shape a person's character. What starts out as a good or innocent common interest (sports, music, gaming) can turn lethal. Paul was simply saying, "Be aware. Don't fool yourself. Choose wisely."

Psalm 1 contrasts the firmly rooted believer with the one who listens to the counsel of the ungodly. The story does not have a happy ending.

"It Won't Happen to Me"

So, why do we cave in to unhealthy influences? What causes us to gradually and unconsciously slip into mediocrity, apathy, and ultimately, a practical denial of the faith we once loved? Is it fear of rejection? Fear of embarrassment? Fear of not being included or missing out? Does caving in under others' influence feed the sinful side of our self-esteem?

When your identity is found through being accepted by others, you will never be able to understand who you really are. You won't be able to discover the person God meant for you to become because you are constantly morphing into someone else, blending into the environment in order to be accepted. Like a chameleon, you change your colors to adapt.

Insecurity also plays a role here, insecurity born out of fear. Critical for every Christian is the ability to stand on your own. And to stand alone, if necessary. God doesn't want you to conform to some cookie-cutter Christian image.

There's only one character image you should ever seek.[3] He wants you to be the unique individual he made you to be. He just doesn't want you to melt like wax when the social heat is turned up.

Difficult? Yes. Impossible? No.

One of Jesus' disciples, Peter, is a good example of this. Peter came across as being very confident. Maybe even arrogant at times. He was a blurter, that guy in the Bible study who always gives the right answer. Type A personality, perhaps. A risk-taker. Competitive. He believed he was strong, but he wasn't. Like some Christians, Peter overestimated his ability to stand. And just when you think you're strong, it's usually at this point that the ground collapses beneath your feet. That's why Paul later warned us to be careful of thinking we're "all that," spiritually.[4]

So, the last night Jesus spent with his disciples, they had dinner, and afterward were walking to a garden to pray. It was a place they had probably been several times before. As they were walking, Jesus said to them, "You will all fall away, for it is written: 'I will strike the shepherd, and the sheep will be scattered.'"[5]

Peter didn't like the way that sounded, especially since Jesus was lumping him in with the rest of those "weak disciples." So he had to say something that would elevate him above the others.

"Even if all [these losers] fall away, I will not."[6] In other words, "Jesus, you've got it all wrong. I mean, I can understand you thinking these bumpkins will totally wig out on you. But it's me. 'Mr. Rock.' It's okay, Lord. I've got your back. You can count on *me*."

Jesus must have been amazed at Peter's lack of insight. Even though he may have had honorable motives, Peter forgot to include something in the equation—himself!

Earlier that evening, Jesus had told his disciples that one of them would betray him. Peter immediately caught John's eye (John was leaning on Jesus).

"*Psst!* John! Ask Jesus which one is the betrayer."

When it was later revealed that Judas was the bad guy, Peter must have felt a sense of relief and affirmation. So when, just a little while later that night, Jesus told them they would all fall away, Peter thought Jesus was confused. So he asserted himself. Unfortunately, Jesus knew more than Peter did, and shot back, "I tell you the truth, today—yes tonight—before the rooster crows twice you yourself will disown me three times."[7]

This was the second time Jesus had informed Peter of his weakness. But he still wasn't getting it. Humility was not a huge character trait for Peter. That's why his unwillingness to be taught by Jesus, brought on by a severe case of self-confidence, prompted Peter to declare, "Even if I have to die with you, I will never disown you!"[8]

Previously overshadowed by Peter's big mouth, all the other disciples chimed in with a hearty "Amen! Us too!"

They were all wrong. But none more so than Peter. Just a little while later, Jesus was arrested in that garden. Peter, once again taking matters into his own hands (this time literally), drew his sword and tried to split a guy's head open like a watermelon on the Fourth of July. He ended up chopping off the man's ear, but Jesus put it back on before being arrested and taken away.

Not long after this, Peter was in a courtyard, warming himself by a fire, when a little servant girl recognized him as one of Jesus' disciples.

He denied it.

Then a maid saw him and said to those standing around, "Hey, everybody. Here's one of those Jesus-followers!"

He denied it again.

Finally, the whole crowd gathered around him, convinced he was a friend of Jesus. This time he started cussing.

And denied he knew Jesus a third time.

That's when the rooster crowed. Guess Peter shouldn't have been so "cocky." In reality, he was a rookie. And a weak one, at that. The truth did eventually sink in through Peter's thick Galilean skull. But it took this memorable trilogy of denial to persuade him. Peter didn't yet know his own sin nature. He hadn't descended into the pit and faced the monster. He hadn't yet realized there was a zombie living inside. Being intimidated and influenced by others was something Peter struggled with. And it's a problem he would face again later on.[9]

That's what the influence of others can do. It doesn't matter how much Scripture you know or how many verses you've memorized. Intimidation can take a Christian who knows a bunch of Scripture and turn him or her into a quivering piece of jelly.

Zombie to Zombie

We traditionally think of "peer pressure" as the stereotypical crowd of bad boys tempting the lone weak person to do something wrong. But seriously, when was the last time a crowd of hooligans tried to pressure you into holding up a bank? Traditional ways of defining peer pressure don't go deep enough. So let's redefine it, taking it to a deeper, more relevant level—beyond just seeing the things we do in life as right and wrong. When we sin, it's more than simply crossing an invisible boundary to the land of badness. In reality, it's our sinful *attitudes* and *choices* that are offensive to God and his character. Our sinful *hearts* disturb him in *his* heart.

God isn't a cold Judge, sitting on heaven's throne, creating laws and rules, rewarding the rule keepers and punishing the rule breakers. Those who believe this have fallen for a colossal lie, a religious fairy tale perpetuated by religious people. God is a moral Being, but that's not the full extent of his character. He is not a one-dimensional god, like some divine automaton or impersonal ruler. Instead, he is a Father who *feels*. The reason we have feelings is because we are made in the image of a God who feels. The Bible describes him as someone who experiences jealousy,[10] anger,[11] love,[12] joy,[13] compassion,[14] sadness,[15] and even grief.[16] To "grieve the Holy Spirit" refers to someone getting his feelings hurt. This doesn't mean that God is wounded like a junior high girl not invited to a birthday party. He isn't petty or shallow with his emotions. For him, being grieved is closer to what a husband feels upon discovering his wife is cheating on him, or vice versa. It's an emotional bruise. A dagger to the heart. And the reason this is so is because when you are in love with someone, you have placed that person close to your heart. You are bonded with him or her. Your life is interwoven with your mate's. And believers in Jesus are described in terms of being the bride of Christ.[17] What could be closer to his heart than us?

So when we stray from Christ in our attitudes or actions, God is understandably saddened. And when he says that bad company corrupts good character, he's referring to the outcome when the sinful nature within one person interacts with the sinful nature in you. From one zombie to another. It's as if the two beings inside are speaking the same language—which they actually are. They are fluent in the language of the "flesh." A sinful social network. And the flesh is weak, insecure, proud, and cowardly. It is also massively arrogant and loves everything God hates.

So when another "zombie" grunts and moans about "fresh

brains" (some sinful attitude or action), the zombie inside you picks up the scent and is very pleased. You give in to the temptation. And God is grieved. Make sense?

Of course, some people are, socially speaking, naturally more independent and self-confident. For them it may be easier to make their own decisions, regardless of what others may think. But even they are not immune.

Peter wasn't. His character caved in under the pressure of a slave girl and the crowd because of his cowardice. It's in those similar moments of temptation that you and I can also forget every promise ever made to God in our deepest moments of intimacy. The passionate love and worship we once experienced fades and seems distant during those times, overshadowed by a new love: for "brains." We long to satisfy the beast within. To feed it. Pacify it.

But we have to ask ourselves, "Is it really worth it?" The predictable, pat answer, of course, is no. So then why do we still allow others to negatively influence us? Because in that moment we choose to love sin and self more than we do Jesus. It feels better to enjoy the acceptance of others than to rest in our acceptance by God. To act out of convenience rather than out of our identity in him. We've lived with our inner zombies all our lives, and we have grown to trust their instincts. Then God comes along and tells us we're not okay and that we should trust *him* instead. That takes a little getting used to. We're not wired to think like that. So when unwise people ask us to walk with them and be their companions in life, it rings true with the selfish beast inside us. It's only later that we understand the stupidity of such a choice.[18] Bad company erodes your good character anytime someone lures you away from being who God wants you to be, or doing something you know God wouldn't want you to do.

So recognize your own weaknesses in this area. Know

yourself. And know and respect the flow and force of the social river nearest your heart. Don't go swimming in the current without the One who is your Life Preserver. And a few good friends.

INFECTED!

Back at work Monday morning, Ben felt refreshed. Unfortunately, deadlines were looming, so he would have to play catch-up. The first face greeting Ben that morning was twenty-eight-year-old Sonya Diaz. Sonya had moved from Miami a few years back with her husband, Ernesto, who runs a local landscaping business. Sonya is proud of her Hispanic heritage, and doesn't hesitate to tell you about it. Brown skin and matching eyes, combined with shoulder-length, midnight-black hair, gracefully crowns her five-foot-three frame.

But more than beauty is packed into this pint-sized woman. Her title at Sk8X is director of operations, but she is much more. Sonya possesses astute organizational skills. And there are plenty of projects to manage at Sk8X. Because the company is small, she wears many hats, and has become the glue that holds Sk8X together.

Besides her and Ben, the magazine employs six others, most under the age of thirty: Rick Masterson, founder, publisher, and editor-in-chief; Scott Sellers, managing editor and director of finance; Philip Griffin, director of marketing and circulation; Jordan Wade, web master and photographer; Robert Jernagin, account and advertising executive; and Kyle Walters, contributing writer, production coordinator, and shipping manager.

The team functions well together. Nobody wants anybody else's job, and *everybody* wants to make more money, especially Rick. And that motivates them all. Occasionally after lunch, though, Kyle will turn up in the storage room, asleep on a pallet of back-issue magazines. Even so, there is a strong work ethic here, and Rick feels confident the magazine is in good hands.

"'Morning, Ben," greeted Sonya. "How was your little vacation?"

"It was good. Spent some time with my family. Crystal and I went to a movie. Took the Frisbee to the park. Mainly just some time to clear my head."

"Aww, honey, I know that must have been rough for you last week. You wanna talk about it?"

In the past few months, Sonya had become sort of a big sister to Ben—in part because she was older, but more so because she had grown up with three older brothers. Her background prepared her to be cooped up with men five days a week. But Ben had also confided in her about his relationship with Crystal, specifically how to understand women.

Still, Ben wasn't ready to reopen last Wednesday's wound just yet. "Maybe sometime," he mumbled, quickly shifting the conversation. "You got any messages for me?"

Sonya laughed. "No, sweetie. I already put all your messages in your work space."

Arriving at his cubicle, Ben discovered a stack of folders in his chair and his computer screen covered in yellow Post-it notes. "Super," he remarked to himself. "I can tell this is going to be an awesome week."

After dropping his shoulder bag to the floor, he moved the stack of folders to his desk and began working through the sticky notes, one by one. Surrounded by a dozen notes was one placed in the center that read:

You can do it, amigo!
—S

Ben worked straight through lunch, snacking on an energy bar from Kyle's drawer while his coworker was "occupied" in the storage room. Before he knew it, the day was gone. Once again, he'd worked way past quitting time.

At 6:15 he heard a buzz. Rummaging through a small mountain of papers, he finally located his vibrating phone. Crystal's face appeared on the caller ID.

"Hey, what's up?" Ben said.

"Hey, you. Where are you? I haven't heard from you all day, and you didn't respond to my texts. You still alive?"

"I'm sorry. I've been slammed here all day, and I'm not even close to finishing."

"Well, I hate to break it to you, Mr. Graphic Designer, but you have plans for tonight."

"*Plans*?" Ben questioned.

"Ben Forman! You better be joking if you know what's good for you."

"I'm kidding. Don't freak. It's our six-month anniversary."

That's when it occurred to Ben that he'd forgotten to buy Crystal a gift, and he was pretty sure she'd be expecting one.

While he was still on the phone, Sonya poked her head inside Ben's cubicle. She had yet another yellow note for him, this one stuck on the tip of her index finger. She dangled it six inches from his face. The note read, in all caps:

HALLOWEEN STAFF DINNER TONIGHT

JAKE'S STEAKHOUSE

7 P.M.

Ben squinted to read the note and then slapped himself on the forehead, silently mouthing an expletive.

"Crystal, hang on a second."

Pressing the mute button, he voiced his frustration to Sonya.

"That's *tonight*? Sonya, I have plans with Crystal this evening. It's our anniversary."

Sonya said, "Congrats. But sorry. Tonight is mandatory, and you gotta be there."

Ben let out a groan.

"What am I gonna do? If I don't take Crystal out, she's gonna kill me! And make no mistake: she *will* kill me."

Sonya tapped a red fingernail on her matching lips, then said, in her Spanish accent, "Okay, I got it. Come to our dinner first, and then take her out later tonight, *or* . . . you could just bring her with you at seven. Ernesto is coming with me, and I'm sure the other guys are bringing their wives or dates."

"Hmm. I know Crystal, and there's no way she's waiting until nine to go out. She's ready to go now. I can almost smell the perfume through the phone. I'll have to sell her on the combined dinner thing. Why is this happening? Just say a prayer she doesn't get emotional."

"First of all, *chico*," Sonya answered, "there is no 'Why?' in life. There is only 'What now?' and you're definitely in the 'What now?' And second, I'll be happy to say a prayer for you."

Ben was about to un-mute his phone, then hesitated. "Oh yeah. One more thing. What are you supposed to get a girl for the sixth-month anniversary?"

Diaz laughed. "You are *such* a guy! Gimme your credit card, and I will call in some flowers and have them delivered to the restaurant. I know a shop that doesn't close till eight."

"That would totally save my life. I really owe you one."

"Ha! You owe me way more than just one. But that's what I get paid for—to think for you men."

Ben pulled his wallet from his back pocket and tossed it to Sonya.

He un-muted his phone, silently mouthing, "Thank you."

• • •

Though the idea of sharing her special night with Ben's coworkers wasn't Crystal's first choice, she surprisingly didn't object.

"All right," Ben announced. "I'll pick you up in forty minutes. Bye."

Ben breathed a sigh of relief. He had dodged a bullet, negotiating his way out of a sticky and potentially volatile situation with Crystal.

On the way to his car, he passed the spot where he'd discovered the corpse less than a week earlier. He chose not to look down the alley. Once home, he took a quick shower, then picked up Crystal.

• • •

Jake's Steakhouse has been a Corazon City tradition for more than twenty-five years, and Ben's family had been there many times. The owner, Jake Wildmon, was in his late sixties but still ran the restaurant that bore his name. His thick, silver hair was usually hidden under a chef's hat—the same hat he'd worn for years. Everybody loved Jake, and his grandfatherly demeanor gave the restaurant a homey ambience. He regularly made trips from the kitchen to the dining area to personally see how his customers were enjoying the food. His white, full-bodied apron and his signature chef's hat were hard to miss. Plus, Jake was a big man—6 feet, 3 inches tall and over 250 pounds.

By the time Ben and Crystal arrived, the rest of the Sk8X crew was already in the small banquet room at the back of the restaurant. They sat down at the end of the table, nearest the door. Ben ordered a steak, and when the food arrived, everyone began eating while simultaneously carrying on multiple conversations across the large table. It was a lively, festive atmosphere with lots of laughter. Just what Ben needed after a long day at work.

Midway through dinner, the restaurant's owner, Jake Wildmon, suddenly appeared, carefully cradling a dozen roses in his arms. "Which one of you pretty young ladies is Crystal?" he inquired in an old, raspy voice.

Everyone's eyes diverted toward where Ben and his girlfriend were sitting. Crystal sheepishly raised her hand. "That would be me," she said.

The party burst into applause.

"Way to go, Ben!" Kyle shouted. "You're the man! Now, where's the ring?"

The arrangement was beautiful—and huge. Ben stared across the table at Sonya, his eyebrows raised in unspoken question. She slowly held up five fingers, then formed an O with her thumb and fingers. Ben's eyes widened. "*Fifty dollars?*" he mouthed.

"They're *beautiful*, baby. Thank you!" Crystal said, kissing him on the cheek.

"It's our six-month dating anniversary," Ben explained.

"Well, I gotta go to the bathroom, everybody," Kyle announced.

"Thanks for sharing, Kyle," Scott said. "That really adds to the moment. You have such a gift."

• • •

The night wore on, and by the time dessert was over, everyone was sufficiently stuffed. Rick tossed a linen napkin onto his empty plate.

"Okay, team, it's getting late, and we do have work in the morning, so I suggest we call it a night. Besides, Walters needs his beauty sleep." Everyone laughed.

"Hey, Masterson. Watch it. I'm a black belt," Kyle joked.

The dinner party was about to get up from their seats when once more, Jake Wildmon appeared through the doorway.

The group paused their chatter.

"More flowers, Jake?" someone quipped.

But Wildmon just stood there, not saying a word. He looked tired, his shoulders slumped. His chef's hat was uncharacteristically crooked, about to fall from his head. His eyes were glazed over, unblinking. His mouth was half-open, his forehead and face beading with sweat.

"Mr. Wildmon, are you okay?" Rick inquired.

A chill swept over the party. Not a soul moved. Crystal clutched Ben's arm with both hands, gripping it tightly.

Rick repeated his question, louder this time. "Mr. Wildmon, sir. Are you all right? Is there something we can do for you?"

The old man stood motionless, staring straight ahead toward the back wall. His eyes had no life in them, like two black portholes leading to nothingness. Suddenly his mouth began quivering, and a whisper escaped. He was trying to speak, but was having trouble forming the words. He slowly licked his lips to moisten them, then swallowed.

"H-hooow . . ." Wildmon's voice was gravelly and hoarse,

127

as if his words were dragging themselves across a dried-up creek bed. The party strained to hear him. Ben and Crystal, still seated, were in closest proximity to him. That's when Ben noticed the meat cleaver in Wildmon's right hand, hanging loosely by his side and covered in blood. Jake's voice increased in volume, struggling to achieve clarity.

"Hooow . . . ahhgh . . . how . . . is . . . your . . . grrr . . . food?"

A dribble of drool escaped his mouth, and Wildmon licked his lips again, only this time running his tongue across them like a hungry man about to eat a juicy steak. With anticipation. And desire. He elevated his head slightly, flaring his nostrils.

Ben dared not speak. Nor did anyone else, with the exception of Rick's wife, who was busy whispering a prayer. It was clear something was horribly wrong with the old man. A huge drop of blood slowly gathered at the meat cleaver's edge and fell to the floor, splattering the white tip of Ben's black Converse. He instinctively jerked his foot away. Then, almost as if orchestrated, the entire party rose from their seats and silently filed past the restaurant owner, who said nothing. Jake Wildmon just stood there, staring at the back wall . . . sweating.

Kyle called 911, and they all left the restaurant.

• • •

The next morning, Ben arrived at work, unrested from the night before. Placing his coffee cup on the work space, he fell back into his chair with a sigh. Promptly propping his feet up, he closed his eyes.

"Ten more minutes of sleep and I'll be ready for this day."

Clasping his hands behind his head, in no time he was asleep. However, the restful experience Ben was hoping for eluded him. Ben Forman was trapped in that familiar no-man's land, the dead space between sleep and consciousness. His mind conjured up dreams, while background office sounds flowed in and out of his subliminal world. His body craved sleep. But keeping his eyes shut felt so good, so Ben relaxed into a quick power nap.

But just minutes in, a noise penetrated his slumber, bursting the bubble of his dream world. Jolted back to the edge of consciousness, he managed enough energy to open one eye. Through his emerging awareness, Ben saw Jake Wildmon standing inside his cubicle. Immaculately dressed in a dark suit, Wildmon wore a white shirt and red tie, stitched with little yellow sailboats. The restaurant owner was clean-shaven and his white hair neatly combed. Ben had never seen him without his chef's hat.

"Mr. Wildmon!" Ben gasped. The shock of seeing him froze Ben with fear in his chair. "Wh-what are you doing here?"

The old man chuckled, placing a hand on his large belly. "Didn't mean to startle you there, son. I just dropped by here to apologize to y'all for my odd behavior last night. I must confess I wasn't feeling quite myself. The wife says I had a touch of fever." He laughed. "But then at my age, these things happen. One day you're fine, next day you've got a dozen ailments and as many pills to take. But that's just old age for ya. You'll be there one day, just you wait. You'll be just like ole Jake here."

Wildmon's laughter and Southern charm put Ben at ease.

Relaxing, Ben slowly lowered his feet from his desk to the floor.

"Yes, sir. And there's no need to apologize, Mr. Wildmon. Us younger folks can feel under the weather sometimes too. It's okay."

Ben was confused, and still sleepy.

"So I thought I'd bring you kids some dinner gift certificates. I left them with that pretty young lady up front. She's real nice."

"Thank you, sir. You didn't have to do that, but still, it's very kind of you."

Wildmon started to walk away, then paused and turned around.

"Ah. Oh yeah, I almost forgot. See what I mean about getting old? Me and Mrs. Wildmon would like to have you over for dinner tonight . . . if you're available, of course."

"Um, me? Dinner? Wh-why me?" Ben inquired.

Wildmon widened his grin. His eyebrows raised, and his countenance altered. "Well, he-he, Ben. Isn't it obvious? Why, I'm going to totally devour your brains tonight, son. Mind if I start now with an appetizer?"

An earthquake of horror shot through Ben's thin frame, catapulting him out of his chair and onto the floor with a thud, causing him to strike his head on a drawer. His coffee sailed off the desk and landed on the hardwood floor, sending a flow of steaming dark roast seeping between the thick pine boards. Ben retreated back under his desk like a frightened animal. He looked up again at Wildmon, but the man had vanished.

"Ben? Hey, Ben! What's going on in here? What the heck are you doing under your desk?" Rick Masterson asked, emerging from his office.

Ben shook his head, blinking his eyes to focus. The young designer now realized it had been a dream. Relieved, though still not fully awake, he yawned, masking the confusing fear still etched on his face.

"Sorry, Rick. I must have dozed off . . . and fallen out of my chair. Whoa. Ha-ha," he said nervously.

"Well, we don't need another snoozing employee around here. Wake up and get off the floor; then meet me in my office, okay? And clean up this mess."

"Sure thing, Rick. Be right there."

Ben stumbled to the restroom and splashed his face with

water. Seeing his reflection in the mirror, he noticed two huge, dark circles under his eyes.

"Who's getting old *now*?" he said to himself. Leaning over the sink, he tried to make sense of what he'd just seen. It seemed so vivid and real. Grabbing a handful of paper towels, he went back to his desk and began sopping up the coffee from the floor. Then he hurried to the glassed corner office Rick Masterson occupied.

"Come in, Ben," Rick said, motioning with his hand. "And shut the door."

Ben took a seat on the overstuffed couch opposite Masterson. He hadn't been in Rick's office since being hired over six months ago, and this made him wonder why he was here. His palms began sweating.

"Ben, you've got these big, dark circles under your eyes. You feeling all right?"

"Yeah, I know. I'm good. I . . . I just didn't sleep much last night, that's all."

"Well, I'm not sure any of us did. That was a bizarre experience, and not one we'll soon forget."

"You got *that* right," Ben replied. "Does anybody know . . . um, have you heard how Mr. Wildmon is doing?"

"I called the hospital first thing this morning," Rick answered. "Ben, Mr. Wildmon died last night. That's all they would tell me. I don't know anything else."

"Woooow," Ben mumbled slowly under his breath.

"'Wow' is right," Rick said, nodding.

"Rick, you think he was . . . becoming one of *them*?"

"Who knows? I mean, you're the expert around here on *that* subject."

Rick's comment struck a nerve, and he could see from Ben's expression that it showed.

"Hey, my bad. That was insensitive," Rick said.

Ben immediately responded, "Nah, Rick. Don't worry about it. It's no big deal."

He was lying.

Rick's comment did bother him. Ben had never fully dealt with the loss of his dad. That unresolved tension, combined with last Wednesday *and* the previous night's experience, was beginning to cause Ben to wonder if he was cursed or something.

Rick broke into his thoughts. "Okay, new subject. That's not why I asked you in here."

Ben felt his heart beating faster. He folded his hands tightly for fear that Rick would see them shaking.

"Are you happy here, Ben?" Rick asked bluntly.

"Wha-what do you mean, am I *happy*?"

"Well, it's not a trick question. I just want to know if you're happy working here at Sk8X. Simple question, that's all."

"Oh." Ben laughed nervously. "Yeah, I like it here. I mean, I'm happy. I enjoy my work a lot."

"I'm really glad to hear that, Ben, because you do excellent work. You have a gift, and you're a great addition to the team."

Ben relaxed his grip and felt the blood circulating back into his fingers.

"Thanks, Rick. I really appreciate that. That means a lot."

"Ben, you've ramped up our magazine's look dramatically. Our market presence is growing, and you're a big part of that, so I'm giving you a raise."

"You serious?" Ben replied enthusiastically. "Thanks, Rick!"

"Well, you deserve it. Okay, then. I guess that's it. Let's get back to work."

Ben got up and was almost to the door when Rick called out to him.

"Hey, let's keep this on the down-low, just between us, okay? And by the way, did you know your shoes don't match?"

Looking down, Ben compared the new black Converse on his right foot to an old, worn-out one on his left foot.

"Yeah, I know," Ben answered. "I misplaced my shoe and had to use this one."

"Well, come payday, you can buy yourself a new pair of shoes," Rick said, laughing.

Ben smiled and nodded.

Outside the publisher's office, Ben spotted Sonya carrying copy paper from the storage room. Seeing him, her face turned anxious, and Ben motioned her into his cubicle.

"So, what was that all about?"

"Nothing, really. He just told me I was doing a great job. Plus . . ." Ben looked around to make sure no one was nearby, then whispered, "He's giving me a raise!"

"Shut *up!*" Sonya said, trying to keep her voice down. "Rick Masterson giving a raise? That's a sure sign of the Apocalypse. Do you know how long it's been since any of us got raises?" Sonya put her paper down and gave Ben a hug. "Amigo! Congrats! Way to go!"

"Pretty cool, huh? But keep it between us, okay?"

"No worries. It's our little secret. So . . ." Diaz continued, "By the way, you've got these big, dark circles—"

"I know, I know. I was at Crystal's till, like, three thirty this morning. She was still emotional after the restaurant incident. Then she disappeared into the bathroom and came out looking all pale. I think the whole experience upset her stomach."

"She'll get over it. Give her a few days."

"I'm not worried. It's typical. But that's why I didn't get to sleep until 4 a.m., and then got up at 7. Hence, these things," he said, pointing to the luggage under his eyes.

Sonya bit her lip, snickering. "You want some of my makeup? We could erase those bad boys right off your face in no time."

"Thanks, but *no* thanks. I'm gonna get back to work now.

Oh, I almost forgot. Rick said Mr. Wildmon passed away last night."

"No *way*!"

"Yeah, it's really sad. That's all we know for now."

Having lost his coffee earlier, Ben opted for an energy drink to help him stay alert. Rick gathered his employees together to tell them about Wildmon. Everyone remained silent, except Kyle Walters, who made another lame attempt at humor.

"You gotta admit, though: it made for a pretty creepy Halloween night, right?"

No one laughed.

At noon, Rick had pizza delivered to help lighten the atmosphere. After work, Ben dropped by Crystal's apartment to check on her. She barely cracked the door open, just enough to say, "Go away!" Ben brushed it off, blaming it on hormones.

The next day, Wednesday, was exactly a week since Ben discovered the body in the alley. He tried not to think about it, keeping his mind occupied instead with work. On Thursday, he arrived at Sk8X to find another yellow sticky note on his computer screen, this one from Rick.

FYI

Jake Wildmon's funeral tomorrow.

*Family receiving guests tonight at
Johnson's Funeral Home.*

R

Ben crumpled the note, tossing it into the trash. He didn't think about it again until driving home that evening. Crystal still wasn't feeling well, and Ben didn't care to be around her anyway. So with nothing else to do that Thursday evening, he decided to pay his respects to Jake Wildmon's family. A gutsy move for a guy who doesn't enjoy crowds that much.

Ben walked into the funeral parlor, then realized he was way underdressed for the occasion. His T-shirt, hoodie, and jeans were hardly appropriate for a funeral visitation.

This is dumb, he thought. *I can't go in there looking like this. I'll send his wife a sympathy card.*

Exiting the funeral home, Ben practically had a head-on collision with a woman.

"Mom?" Ben asked. "What are *you* doing here?"

"I think it's me who should be asking *you* the same question," Patricia Forman said, hugging her youngest son.

"I-I just thought I would come pay my respects to Mrs. Wildmon, since Dad used to take us to Jake's a lot."

"That's very sweet of you, honey. I'm sure Debra appreciated your stopping by."

"Well, I didn't exactly go in yet. I just realized I'm not dressed right, so I'm just gonna send her—"

"Nonsense," his mother said, cutting him off. "You'll be just fine . . . Ben, your *shoes*!"

"I know. Don't worry about it, Mom," Ben answered.

"Just tell me this isn't the latest fad."

"Mom, please!"

"Oh, never mind. Debra Wildmon raised four boys. Trust me; she'll understand. Besides, you're with me. Come on. It's cold out here," his mom said, hooking her arm around her son's.

Ben wasn't going to say no to his mother, or persuade her of any opinion but her own. Inside, the room overflowed with flower arrangements sent by sympathetic friends. Several people were visiting with Mrs. Wildmon, most dressed in regular clothes . . . just not quite as regular as Ben's.

Patricia went to Jake's widow, giving her a warm embrace.

"Debra, we're so sorry for your loss. Jake was a great man.

This whole town is gonna miss him." Ben stood by his mom, saying nothing. He could feel his hands sweating again.

"Thank you both for coming," she said with a grateful smile. "Everyone has been so nice. I know my darkest days are ahead of me, but my boys and their families are here, so I know that'll help."

Patricia clutched Debra's hands. "If there's anything we can do, don't hesitate to call."

"I'm okay, but if you know anyone over at the hospital or police department . . . I can't get much information from either of them. They said Jake had a massive aneurism on the way to the emergency room, and by the time he got to the hospital, there was nothing they could do. And the coroner took forever to release his body."

"I don't understand," Patricia responded. "Why would the police be involved?"

"Something about Jake resisting while being taken to the hospital. They said he had a seizure and became combative. But Jake wasn't like that. I don't know. I just want some answers, but right now my hands are full with family and this funeral."

Patricia didn't know what to say, so she just hugged Debra Wildmon again. At the end of the room was the open casket. Patricia walked over to see Wildmon's body. Ben started to leave when his mom motioned him over.

"It's not polite to leave without viewing the body," she whispered.

Ben stood by his mom. Though he tried to resist, he couldn't help looking at the body. "He looks so natural," Patricia said, loud enough for those around her to hear.

Naturally dead! Ben thought.

A grandmotherly figure standing behind Ben commented, "I always liked his hair. You know, it used to be dark brown. I knew him back then. Still a handsome man, even at his . . . *our* age. And look what a pretty tie he's wearing!"

That's when Ben noticed it. A red tie, stitched with little yellow sailboats . . . exactly like his dream earlier that morning.

"I gotta go, Mom."

Ben quickly left the room and disappeared into the night.

● ● ●

Later that evening, a second-floor window opened at Ben's apartment complex, and a black Converse sneaker flew out of the opening. Sailing across the parking lot, it landed inside a Dumpster.

Chapter 8

ZOMBIE RULES

The true hypocrite is the one who ceases to perceive his deception. The one who lies with sincerity.

—Andre Gide

In later times some will abandon the faith and follow deceiving spirits and things taught by demons.

—The Apostle Paul, in 1 Timothy 4:1

Promises, Promises

Something happened to me at age sixteen that forever changed my life. One summer Sunday afternoon, I was driving home from a buddy's house. Another friend of mine was in the car with me. Two teenage hippie boys, decked in blue jeans and flannel shirts. And barefoot. Go figure. It had just begun to drizzle rain a few minutes earlier, and I turned onto a country road headed back toward town.

As we traveled down this long hill, we came near a bend in the road. Coming up the hill pretty fast was this guy on a motorcycle. And for some unknown reason, as he rounded the bend, he lost control of his bike and began a sideways slide toward me. But while skidding up the country road, he separated from his bike and tumbled head over heels into a ditch. The motorcycle, however, continued an accelerated slide toward me, eventually slamming hard into the driver's side door. The impact of the collision sent hundreds of glass bits shooting across the interior of the car. I did the only thing my sixteen-year-old mind knew to do: instinctively stomp the brake pedal as hard as I could. We skidded down the wet pavement for what seemed like forever, eventually coming to rest just off the road.

My brain kicked into overdrive, sending lightning-fast signals to my body, doing a "system check" to see if everything was still functioning properly. After processing what had just happened, I checked to see if my friend was hurt. We both checked out fine. Glass was everywhere, though, and I later found it down my shirt and in my front pocket. Glass was also all over the floor, which would soon make for a cautious barefoot exit from the car. Once I knew I was still alive and all right, my adrenaline temporarily subsided. But I was jolted back to a state of panic when my friend screamed, "DUDE, YOU'RE ON TOP OF HIM!"

Apparently, as I slid down the road, I had come to rest in the same ditch the man had rolled into. I immediately threw the gears into reverse and spun up the hill about ten feet, inadvertently running over the man a second time. Again, my mind was thrust into hyper-speed thought. I fast-forwarded and saw a future labeled with words like "manslaughter" and "jail time." I pictured myself in one of those orange prison jumpsuits. My future had officially been canceled.

And that's when it happened. I got religious. Since I wasn't a churchgoer, I didn't exactly know how the game was played. But I did know that people prayed to God, asking him for help when they got in trouble. And I was definitely in trouble. BIG trouble. My pulse was beating like a speed-metal drummer on a kick drum. So out of pure fear, I prayed. No, make that,

I *begged*. I began making deals with God in my head while kicking my jammed-shut door. I promised God that if he got me out of this mess, I would stop my sinful behavior. I told him I would clean up my act, that I wouldn't hang out with bad influences anymore. Promise after promise I made as I shoulder-slammed and kicked my way out of the car.

"God, just don't let this man be dead. Please! Please don't let him die!"

Finally, the door flew open, again sending more glass spraying my way. We jumped out barefoot onto the wet pavement and ran down the hill. Arriving at where the man was, we saw him lying motionless in the ditch. Then, unexpectedly, he started moving and slowly stood to his feet.

"Oh my gosh! M-mister, are you all right, sir? Are you hurt?" I yelled.

Brushing the damp dirt off of his jacket, the man looked up at the two teenage hippies, blinked his eyes, and responded, "Yeah, I think . . . I think I'm fine."

And he was. In fact, he was more than fine. Amazingly, this man did not have one single scratch on his body. Unhurt in the crash. Unscathed in the slide across the road. Unbruised in the violent collision with the ditch. And unharmed by having a car land on top of him and getting run over by it twice.

Not a single scratch.

His motorcycle was another story. And so was my car. The man pushed his bike up the road to his house about a mile away while I drove slowly alongside him, holding my door on with my left arm. Later that day, I remembered all those things I had said to God during our in-car negotiations. I had sworn to get religious and stop doing bad things. I had even considered going to church or performing some kind of devout duty. And I did okay for a couple of weeks. Then something started happening inside. A force greater than post-crash promises began raising its ugly head. Something inside of me no longer cared about God or promises made to him in a moment of panic and fear. All it cared about was self-preservation and getting bailed out of catastrophe. The ink on my inner contract with God had hardly dried before beginning a fast fade. Soon it would disappear altogether. Fortunately for me, within a month or so, another friend entered my life. And what I saw in him made me thirsty. This teenage guy knew Jesus, and in a short time he introduced me to him.

Faux Faith

Looking back, it was that incident that introduced me to the danger and deception of being religious. Someone has described religion as "man's attempt to reach God." That rings true with me. I mean, think about the religious stuff we've invented to help people make a connection with their Creator. In some religions, there are required places to visit, special wheels to spin, dead people to appease, sacrifices to make, and good deeds to perform. And even within Christianity, a pervasive religious odor lingers in the air. We have a litany of religious activity. Sunday morning performances we put on for the sake of God and others, hoping for his applause or a heavenly "Amen!"

Religious stuff.

There are liturgies we observe. Services we attend. Special prayers we pray. A certain percentage of money we give. Verses to memorize. Meetings and studies we commit to. Duties to discharge. Religious tasks to complete. In some churches, even certain clothing is considered more appropriate for "worship," as if God is so shallow as to care about worldly social protocol and American fashion. I'm sure he appreciates us reducing him to this level.

Things were no different in Jesus' day. The Son of God was surrounded by a clan of religious leaders who had also messed things up in a major-league way. One way they did this was through their teaching (more about that in another chapter). But the other way they perverted things was by their *example*, turning faith into a religious circus.

Jesus, not known for being a wimpy man, wasn't afraid to inform the crowds that their religious leaders were a total sham and unworthy of being followed. In one message, recorded for us by a former cheating tax collector named Matthew, Jesus began by revealing: "Everything they do is done for men to see."[1] *Really, Jesus? Everything? Are you serious?* Apparently so.

According to Jesus in Matthew 23:6, these guys were a total facade. Counterfeits. Fakes. Actors. Had there been the Academy Awards back then, they would have won the Oscar for "Best Performance by a Group of Phonies." They weren't who they appeared to be. And Jesus intentionally exposed them for who they really were. He crashed their party. And that made them very, very uncomfortable . . . and also angry. Angry enough to want to kill him.

And what did Jesus find so wrong with what they were doing? Weren't they the guardians of the truth? Didn't they perform their religious duties faithfully? Didn't they pray? Didn't they read the Bible? Didn't they lead? Didn't they look and act the part of godly leaders?

Yes.

They also memorized tons of Bible verses, even tying little boxes of scripture cards to their arms and foreheads— you know, so everyone could see how religious and godly they were. They knew more Bible than you, and made sure you were aware of this fact. And they liked how this made them feel. Superior. Special. Sacred. They committed Scripture to memory, not because they loved God or his Word, but in order to be noticed by others.

They also loved the place of honor they enjoyed in their religious subculture and being greeted with respect in the marketplace. This kind of attention fed their egos and tossed a bowl of brains to their inner zombies every time someone called one of them "Rabbi." They liked recognition (v. 6). Being called "leaders" exalted them, making them feel important (v. 12).

Long prayers were another part of their religious game, and they composed some really good ones in public, giving the impression that they were spiritual (v. 14). But in reality, they were blind to the truth—about God and about themselves (v. 16). They did "religious stuff" but ignored the things God really cares about most—like justice, mercy, and faithfulness (v. 23)—heart attitudes that translate into outward actions, but usually in ways that no one sees. And if no one sees you being religious, then your ego can't be fed. And that's no fun.

Jesus said these men looked good on the outside, but on the inside was rampant self-indulgence (v. 25). He called them "whitewashed tombs," inside of which were "dead men's bones" (v. 27). No real spiritual life there. These guys were literally the "walking dead." They appeared outwardly righteous (v. 28), and as such believed they were somehow better than the heathen and those "other" believers (vv. 29–32).

Then Jesus landed the knockout punch. More than fakes. More than hypocrites. "In reality," Jesus was saying, "you men are snakes, sons of vipers." And to a Jewish mind, that was the equivalent of saying you were pure evil. "And what's more," he added, "you're all going to hell" (v. 33, paraphrased). Okay, so Jesus, tell us what you *really* feel!

Fortunately for us, the Lord was a great communicator. He always meant what he said and said what he meant. He understood that religion is merely a costume temporarily masquerading the zombies within us. For you and me, Christian activity and service can easily be that costume. We attempt to keep our inner zombies' mindless hunger moans quiet through religiosity and Christian endeavor. The more we do for God, the less our sinful cravings will be heard, right?

Nope.

It's actually just the opposite. Christian service (mission trips, singing in the choir, mowing the church lawn, going to Bible studies, attending fellowship gatherings, helping the homeless, attending more church services, etc.) may fill up your schedule, preventing you from having time to get yourself in trouble. But it has zero effect on causing your sinful self to get any better. The danger is that you will start feeling really good about yourself as you do all these things. And that good feeling begins to swell, producing pride and a feeling of superiority over others who don't serve the way you do. And you gradually morph into a Pharisee without even knowing it.

But sad to say, by being religious we also sometimes gain greater acceptance with the Christian crowd. And as a result we assume our standing with God is improved as well. Even servanthood can be twisted to serve the self-god. The more I serve, the more I am committed. The more I am committed, the better I am. The better I am, the better off I am in God's eyes (and thus better than you). It's a subtle process, but it's all too common. This is exactly why Jesus advised us to be careful about parading our service to God in order to be seen by men. Instead, he urged us to practice our faith "in secret" without a public audience.[2] Serving in obscurity is no fun for self, especially when others get all the attention. But it helps us avoid the trap of trying to please God, and you're back to earning/working for your salvation again. And that also feeds your ego-driven zombie.

Faith in Jesus just doesn't seem to be enough these days. We subconsciously feel that we need the "extras." Your inner zombie wants to "help" you in your relationship with Jesus. But it's a trick. It knows that by adding self-effort, it will feel good about itself and grow in its control over you. You may be insulated from a host of sins through serving God, but the subconscious attitude of "Look at me. Look how spiritual I am. Look how I serve God," along with the subtle pride, is epidemic in churches. And among Christian leaders.

All of this is merely an attempt to achieve a clear conscience that assures us everything is okay between God and us.[3]

Another reason these good works can be dangerous is because Jesus has already pleased God for you. When he cried out, "It is finished" on the cross, he meant that your debt to God was now paid.[4] "It is finished" is one word in the New Testament's original language, meaning "Paid in full." Jesus satisfied God's righteous demands because you never could.[5]

You struggle with sin, so you "try harder." You fail. So you try even harder. You add more service and activities. You make promises. You "do" more for God. And why? To keep you from screwing up again and because you really want to live for him. But there are other forces at work here too. Hidden motivations that elude us. In reality, we try harder because of the "buzz" it gives our inner zombies. Every time we attempt to satisfy God through religious service or deeds, we throw a bucket of brains down that hole. And the flesh junkie in each of us reanimates all over again, becoming stronger and more confident. And harder to kill. It doesn't at all mind dressing up like a clean, committed Christian as long as it can still be fed daily.

Ironic, really, how the whole point of Jesus' work in us is to save us from sin's ditch and a futile religious lifestyle. And yet, like a car whose front end is out of line, we constantly drift and slide toward that ditch.

Church activity and religious works can't mask the scent of the rotting corpse below. Just like the Pharisees. Avoid their example.

I wonder what Jesus would say if he walked into the average church this Sunday morning. Would he find a swarm of service? A buzz of activity? Imagine for a moment there's no stage or platform. No ambient lighting. No concert venue. No theater atmosphere. No big screens. No Broadway stage-show sets. What if we scratched all that for a few months and simply came together as the body of Christ? What if we chucked the religious stuff and came as broken followers, sick of being entertained, seeking instead to encounter him and love one another, no matter who saw us do it?

What if we shed our religious suits, exposing the zombie for who he really is. And what if we do all this, not to gain any acceptance from God, but simply because we already are fully accepted by him?

Imagine that.

Why So Serious?

But there's another subtle trick our zombies play on us. In an attempt to tame our sinful nature, many Christians buy into a system of thought that believes that the more rules you have, the "godlier" you are. If you have a spiritual problem, the best way to resolve it is to simply create a regulation for yourself. A standard. You just need a new habit, or new set of habits. Replace old, bad behavior with good behavior. If you can submit control of your life to a moral code, you can beat your problems and defeat the enemy within.

The only flaw in this approach is that both Jesus and Paul said it just doesn't work.

"Wait a minute," someone says. "I know lots of fine,

upstanding Christian people who live by God's rules, and their lives are very Christlike and worthy of imitation. Are you saying the rules don't work for them?"

No. I'm saying that's what Jesus and Paul said. These people's lives may be morally upright, but according to the apostle Paul, and Christ himself, rules are only effective in dealing with *outward* behavior, not the condition of the heart. Allow me to explain.

As we have already seen, the wickedness of our sin nature is corrupt and unchanging. It can't be reformed or made better. It only grows worse and worse, continuing to horribly malfunction.

Let's say you got mad and punched some guy in the face. He called the police, and they arrested you, placing you in handcuffs. Now you can't punch him anymore. But that doesn't resolve the issue of *why* you punched him in the first place. The anger that caused you to knock the guy's lights out is still inside you. And even the police can't handcuff your mind or emotions. A night in jail or a hefty fine may prevent you from doing something foolish again, but the anger that caused it may simmer inside you for years.

Some psychologists say that if you perform a certain healthy behavior long enough, it becomes a habit and your life is changed. And while that may work in dieting, studying, or exercise, it still can't change your heart. The heart and mind are a battlefield. When God changes the way you look at life, fulfillment, pleasure, relationships, and solving problems, your behavior will also change. Heart and mind first, then behavior.

Don't misunderstand: some rules can help curb sinful behavior. But that's not good enough for God, who's way more concerned with your heart and mind. Genuine change is from the inside out, not the other way around.

So if the rules can't help our hearts, why did God put so many commands in the Bible? Why would he give us rules if they're useless? What's the point? To answer these questions we first have to make a distinction between God's rules and man's rules. One of Jesus' biggest problems with the religious leaders of his day was that they not only perverted God's commands, making them say stuff God never intended them to say, but they also made up their own set of rules as well. Sort of "extra credit" stuff. But over time *their* rules became as serious and binding as Scripture itself. We do the same thing today. We take Scripture out of context and make it condemn things in our culture that *we* deem inappropriate. Depending on the particular church or Christian group, these rules vary. For example, Paul told the Thessalonians to "abstain from all appearance of evil."[6] Someone may read this verse and conclude that since the topic of zombies deals with flesh-eating, it is therefore inappropriate and evil. Henceforth this book is evil. Oops!

But Paul didn't say, "Abstain from everything in life that some random Christian might believe is inappropriate." Doing this is not only unbiblical; it's also ignorant and impractical. You can find Christians who'll object to anything—movies, the Internet, eating meat, wearing designer clothes, having a nice car, or playing the electric guitar.

Truth is, there are hundreds of morally neutral issues we face that fall into the category of "gray areas." But instead of throwing up a wall of concrete rules, the wise follower of Jesus will seek him and his Word regarding the issue. He will learn to rely on the Holy Spirit within and walk with him in a genuine relationship. If all you have are rules to guide you, then you don't need (or even have) a relationship with Jesus. But the budding Pharisee will simply make a rule and move on. His behavior may change, but his sinful heart remains the same.

Apparently both Jesus and Paul got very upset when people perverted God's commands and made up their own rules, so it's worth reviewing what they said on the subject.

We would all agree that obeying God's rules can't save us or get us to heaven (Galatians 1:6–9; 3:24; 5:1–4). That's because God's rules were never *intended* to save us (Galatians 3:23–25). His Law was meant to serve as our "tutor," leading us to Christ (Galatians 3:24). His righteous standards only demonstrate our inability to obey them. But why would he give us rules he knew we couldn't keep perfectly all the time? So we'd realize our need for a Savior and cry out to him (Romans 8:3–4).

Paul said that if you could get to heaven by keeping the rules, then you wouldn't need Jesus (Galatians 5:1). Christ set us free from having to keep the Law, not to have us become enslaved to it all over again. Furthermore, your chances of earning your way to heaven are about as likely as a corpse running a marathon!

Paul went on to tell the Galatian Christians that if they trusted in their ability to earn God's favor through keeping his Law, then Jesus would be of no benefit to them (v. 2). Salvation is found in Christ alone—plus *nothing*. You can't keep some of God's rules and not keep all of them. It's all or nothing with God (v. 3). You have to keep every one of God's standards perfectly for your whole life to achieve perfection before God. And even then, you would still fall short because of the sin virus within you. And if you try to combine rules with grace as a means to gain salvation, you will forfeit, or lose, grace (v. 4). The only way to "fall from grace," Paul said, is by refusing to completely trust in that grace. Grace is the only road to salvation. Keeping the rules is a dead end.

So what is our hope of achieving righteousness before God? It's *faith*. Complete and exclusive trust in Jesus Christ alone. Do you really get that?

And what about *after* you trust Jesus? What part do God's commands play then? Most Christians will accept that salvation is by grace through faith, but somehow our good standing with God is maintained by obeying the rules. Not so, according to the apostle Paul.

Keeping a list of dos and don'ts cannot cleanse your heart from sin or make you holy. To think otherwise is to let a zombie sneak up on you. External standards can't cure you from self-centeredness, but they can give you a severe case of self-righteousness. And that actually displeases God most. It is deception to equate self-denial with spirituality. Paul wrote to the Colossians that keeping religious rules is futile, even though these rules "have an *appearance of wisdom*."[7] In reality, they have no value or power to kill your inner zombie.[8]

God doesn't equate our standing before him with certain external measurements, *no matter how good they sound*. If spirituality is nothing more than simply obeying a list of "Do this" and "Don't do that," then any disciplined person can be spiritual. But godliness goes much deeper than being strong willed or disciplined. Look at the Pharisees. They kept a lot of good rules, but missed it all when it came to God. Being disciplined can *promote* growth, but it can't cause it. The change you need was settled by what Jesus did for you at the cross—nothing more, nothing less, and nothing else. It was his righteousness, not yours, that purchased your salvation and won your freedom. He did for you what you never could have done for yourself.

"Wait. So is it useless to read my Bible every day?" Of course not. But does God command us to have a quiet time or devotion every morning at seven? Does it have to last at least thirty minutes, with ten minutes spent in prayer? Must it include a notebook, several colored pens, a spiritual journal, and a commentary? No. Can all those things be helpful? Yes. Are they required? Nope.

Is It Party Time, Then?

As a result of Christ's accomplishment at the cross, God now views you as holy. That fact is established by him and will never change (2 Corinthians 5:21). He now sees you clothed with the righteousness of Jesus himself. Think about it! Your standing before God is forever fixed, based on Jesus' work and accomplishments, not yours. Self-denial cannot improve your righteous position in Christ. How could we ever think we could improve on the salvation God himself has already provided for us? There is no Christian deed you or I can do that will motivate God to make us more holy or acceptable in his sight. No act of obedience can in any way improve your standing before him. In fact, even obedience means nothing to God unless it is motivated by grace and love out of a relationship with Jesus Christ. He wants your heart first and foremost.[9]

I see this in many young people today who have grown up in Christian homes, but bear little or no resemblance to the God their parents claim to worship. They received the facts about God from nursery school to high school. They attended all the retreats, camps, and mission trips. But upon arriving at college, they began making their own decisions about life. And God often gets the boot. That's because facts are not the same as faith. Hearing about someone's experience with God is not the same as experiencing him yourself. You have to "own" your own faith.

As a Christian, no matter what you do, you will never be any more loved or accepted by God than you were at the moment you received Christ. Are there commandments in Scripture? Of course. Lots of them. Does God have standards of thought and conduct that he commands us to obey? Obviously. Absolutely. Yes! But God's commandments must be understood in a context of relationship love, not law. Our devotion to Christ is a willing one, not one born out of obligation or duty. Jesus said, "If you love me, you will obey what I command."[10] Notice, first comes the love; then comes the obedience. Of course God wants us to do what is right, even if we're not feeling emotionally in love with him at the moment. But he prefers that we obey him out of a loving relationship and heart for him, not out of a cold compulsion to "keep the rules." Unfortunately for some, the rules are just another opportunity to feel good about themselves and earn God's approval, boosting their self-righteous image. Have you ever fallen into this trap? Have you ever embraced this myth as truth?

If you degrade your relationship with God into merely coloring within the lines and keeping the rules, the beast in the pit wins—and the religious monster within will convince you you're something that you're not, creating a false sense of spirituality. You'll be proud, with a counterfeit feeling of moral superiority.

You'll take minor subjects and make them more important than they actually are. You'll say things the Bible never says, and make issues of all the wrong things.

You'll have a judgmental and critical spirit—the worst form of Pharisaism (Matthew 23:13–15).

You'll stunt your growth in Christ. You'll have a warped view of God as a Father who is never pleased with you.

You'll be eaten up with frustration because you're still living in your own power. And you'll continue to struggle with sin inside.

You'll never experience real freedom in Christ, because legalism is the enemy of grace and wisdom. You'll live in a constant state of fear that you'll abuse your freedom, and out of this fear you'll use rules (or God's rules misapplied) to keep yourself in check.

You'll never have any real peace because you can never be sure if God is happy with you. You'll never be "good enough." There will always be some minor rule or command you've missed.

And you'll be way too busy stressing over whether you have been good enough today to really enjoy the life God intended you to have. Sound fun?

Again, keeping the rules cannot produce holiness (Mark 7:15, 21–22). It cannot restrain fleshly desires (Colossians 2:19–23). And it cannot set you free from sin (Acts 15:10; Galatians 5:1).

Believing that obeying the commandments protects you from your sin nature is like building a fence in the backyard to keep the neighbor's air out. It's not only ineffective; it's also stupid.

But equally damaging is the "All right, let's party, then!" attitude. Seriously, this is the worst form of grace abuse. God gave us *liberty*, not *license*. We were freed *from* sin, not freed *to* sin. That's why some of the New Testament writers gave us powerful reminders. For example:

> Do not use your freedom as a cover-up for evil.
> —Peter[11]

We are now free to enjoy and live for Jesus, not to sin (2 Corinthians 5:15). We serve a new and wonderful Master now!

"You, my brothers [and sisters], were called to be free," wrote Paul. "But do not use your freedom to indulge the sinful nature."[12]

Our freedom does not include the right to serve or feed the zombie. Instead, now we can actually obey God, whereas before we were totally unable to (Romans 8:6–7). (Elsewhere Paul wrote to the Corinthians, "Don't let your liberty cause others to stumble."[13])

God passionately desires our hearts. He wants our love. And where there is love, obedience has a way of becoming real and regular. This love casts out the fear of not pleasing God.[14] In fact, love will cover a lot of things in your life.[15]

And it will turn your religion into relationship.

Episode Nine

TAMING THE LIVING DEAD

Leaving the funeral home, Ben decided he'd had enough weirdness for one day. He'd also had enough comments about his mismatched shoes. So he stopped by the mall and purchased a new pair of black Converse All-Stars. When he arrived at his apartment, Ben jerked open the freezer door and scanned the sparsely populated compartments, eventually selecting a box of pizza bites. After tossing them in the microwave, he grabbed the remote and dove for the couch. Ben's simple agenda that evening: eat, watch TV, and avoid anything *dead*—dead *people*, dead *things*, and especially the *living* dead. But true to his luck, the first thing on TV was an infomercial advertising an herbal supplement "guaranteed to curb the effects of the Z-38 virus." Advertisements like this are typically found in tabloids, usually endorsed by washed-up celebrities and targeting mainly an older demographic. None of these "remedies" has ever been proven effective. Since 1994, the National Drug Administration has required every such product to include a warning label that reads:

This product has not been approved by the NDA and therefore is NOT CLINICALLY TESTED or medically proven to reverse the effects of the Z-38 virus.

Or in common language, *Take at your own risk, 'cause this stuff is for entertainment purposes only.*

This warning came about as the result of a 1992 high-profile lawsuit in which an Arizona woman named Margaret Kilbeck overdosed on Z-GONE, a "miracle pill" manufactured by Lassiter Laboratories. The large capsule contained extracts from cactus plants, mushrooms, Chinese herbal roots, and a "Patented Mystery Ingredient." Lassiter Labs claimed that after "decades of research" they had uncovered the hidden location of the Z-38 virus in the human genome. They boasted that this discovery came in cooperation with the National Institute for Genome Research. It was later uncovered that one of Lassiter's "scientists" had merely been a lab assistant at the National Institute. Even more disturbing, it turns out that Z-GONE's "mystery ingredient" was, in reality, a strain of the Z-38 virus itself.

An investigation subsequently revealed that Lassiter had smuggled zombie parts, purchased on the black market from the former Soviet Republic of Uzmenistan. Every person who took Z-GONE (*all* eight hundred) eventually experienced the full-rage force of Z-38. The common denominator in their infections and deaths was the Lassiter Laboratories product. Mrs. Kilbeck, then forty-nine, mistakenly doubled her dose of the product, shortly thereafter developing an unsightly rash on her neck and face. That's when she contacted a local personal injury attorney, who filed a lawsuit. However, before she got her day in court, Mrs. Kilbeck suddenly lost all control of her faculties during a routine doctor's visit. She attacked and killed her family physician, a nurse, and two patients in the waiting room. These soon reanimated and were terminated. Kilbeck herself was shot outside a Laundromat a short time later.

This unfortunate incident motivated authorities to follow through with her case. They located Lassiter Laboratories in a seedy dockside district of Hoboken, New Jersey. It turned out to be just an old warehouse teeming with rats. Inside, investigators found file cabinets, computers, a makeshift laboratory, and an assembly line of tables. The company's owner, Demitri Rakmelevich, was arrested and charged with over eight hundred counts of negligent homicide. He's currently serving multiple life sentences in a maximum-security Jersey prison.

As a result of this high-profile case, all products similar to Rakmelevich's are required to display the government's warning label. Most of these concoctions are harmless mixtures of fruits, spices, and sugar.

But there are also other widely advertised "preventative cures" for Z-38, including exercise DVDs, meditation regimens, diet plans, therapeutic detoxification massages, herbal baths, magic stone therapy, light treatment, behavior-modification camps, hypnosis, and a host of religious remedies. Many fall for these misleading marketing schemes. Desperate people will try just about anything for a dose of hope. In reality, these products prey on fear, banking on the anxieties of a gullible public.

Not Ben Forman, though. He knows there's no magic cure for Z-38. This virus is an inseparable part of our humanity, he'd tell you. Science can split the atom, but it has yet to identify that invisible line separating our dignity from our depravity. It's the curse we live with, and what makes it come alive is anybody's guess. Ben's plan is to simply steer clear of anything related to those monsters.

And hope they don't one day come after him.

• • •

After watching TV for a while, Ben prepared for bed. While brushing his teeth, he received a text.

```
Hey, u still up? Can u talk a sec? :)
```

Ben rolled his eyes and groaned. He was tired and didn't feel like engaging in another dramatic episode with his girlfriend. Her last words to him had been "Go away!" but her text indicated she might be in better spirits now. He reluctantly decided to respond.

```
Heading to bed, but I can talk for a
         few. Want me to call?
```

Crystal:

```
Uh-huh.
```

Ben called her number.

"Hey, what's up? How are you feeling?"

"I'm okay, I guess. I've missed you," she whined.

"Yeah, you too," Ben replied. "Sorry. I've been super busy at work, and I thought you might need some time to yourself."

"I've still got a fever. And I'm lonely. Why haven't you called me?"

This was exactly the kind of thing that drove Ben crazy.

"Hel-*lo*. Crystal? Didn't you hear what I just said? Besides, when I came over the other day, you practically bit my head off. You *do* remember doing that, right?"

"Kinda. But you could've called to check on me. What if I was dead?"

Ben was frustrated with his girlfriend, and nothing he said made her happy. Obviously, the impact from Monday's roses was overshadowed by the weird encounter at Jake's and Ben's distance since then.

"Okay, Crystal. I apologize for not calling you. How's that sound?"

"Sounds like you don't mean it. Like you're reading from a script."

"Come on, Crystal. Tell me what you want me to do. What would make you happy?

"If you came over . . ."

"What? Tonight? Crystal, it's late, and I have an early morning. Besides, I haven't been sleeping too well lately. I'll come over tomorrow, okay?

"You don't care about me anymore, do you?" she complained.

"That's ridiculous. Stop being immature. I do care about— Hello? Crystal? . . . Perfect!"

Ben turned off the bedside lamp and called it a day.

● ● ●

Friday morning, Ben felt rested, waking up with renewed energy. He hit his cubicle like a man on a mission. By noon his stomach was craving food. He called Crystal, hoping she was in a better mood.

"Hey, you. Feeling better today? Can I take you to lunch?"

"Yes I am, and duh! I'm starving!"

Ben scratched his head, concluding that he'd never be able to figure out the opposite sex.

"Okay, I'll be there in fifteen. Bye."

Ben grabbed his jacket and headed for the door. That's when Kyle Walters intercepted him.

"Hey, man," Kyle said. "Where you going?"

"Just heading downtown for some lunch with Crystal," Ben responded.

"Cool! Mind if I join you?"

At just twenty-four, Kyle was already a legend of sorts, with three unofficial titles: (1) daredevil skateboarder, because he'd attempt almost anything, with the scars to prove it; (2) professional napper—the storage room being his second office; and (3) king of the one-liners—what with his awkward, overconfident remarks and all. Kyle routinely inserted himself into conversations or situations where he wasn't invited.

"Well, Kyle, actually Crystal and I were going to meet for—"

"Awesome! I'll get my jacket. Be right back, bro!"

Though a bit obnoxious, Kyle's amiable personality and boyish smile made him hard to resist. Walters returned so quickly that Ben didn't have time to mount a defense or change his mind. And though lunch with Kyle as the third wheel wasn't on Ben's agenda, he found himself giving in.

The trio ate burgers at an old diner downtown, with Kyle dominating the conversation. Crystal actually thought it funny, mainly because he talked mostly about nothing. At one point, she scribbled a note on her napkin, secretly sliding it across the table to her boyfriend.

> *Neglected as a small child? Raised by wolves?*
> *No human contact?*

Ben covered his mouth to conceal the laughter.

● ● ●

Afterward they were all walking to the car when Crystal spotted a handbag through a store window.

"Ben, can we go in and see how much it costs?" she asked.

"Well, I really need to get back—"

"Sure we can," blurted Kyle, opening the door.

Crystal entered the store, whereupon she threw herself into shopping mode. Meanwhile, Ben and Kyle waited uncomfortably near the intimate fashions section. Not far from them were two people—a man and a woman—arguing. The woman was actually a teenage girl—about 5 feet, 9 inches tall with shoulder-length red hair and green eyes. She was wearing jeans and a bright green V-neck sweater. The man was older, perhaps in his late forties. Their verbal confrontation escalated, growing louder and more intense. The man tried to calm the teenager down, but the more he tried, the worse it got.

Then the girl's voice reached the shouting stage.

"You don't get it! I *want* this dress, and that's all that matters. I don't care what you say anymore. It's my life, and I'll do whatever I want. This is not about you. It's about ME! It's *my* birthday, you insensitive creep! I hate you!"

Her shouting attracted everyone's attention in the store. A salesclerk called for security. Then the girl began screaming, cursing wildly. She turned over a rack of clothes, and the man attempted to restrain her. Wrestling free from his hold, she leapt on his back, wrapping her legs tightly around his waist. Ben and Kyle watched in amazement, waiting for someone to do something. But they all stood by in group shock as the drama in front of them unfolded.

Then unexpectedly, the red-haired teenager bit the side of the man's neck. Writhing her head back and forth like a lion tearing meat off its prey, she gnawed off a huge chunk of flesh. Spitting it out, she dove in for another bite. Crystal dropped the handbag and bolted for the front of the store, screaming as she ran. She was followed by Ben and everyone in the store.

Everyone, that is, except Kyle.

Walters stood motionless, fascinated with the scene being played out before him. The adrenaline junkie found the whole episode quite entertaining. Then he did the unthinkable. He approached the wild-eyed girl.

Still chewing a mouthful of flesh, she released her leg grip and jumped down off the wounded man, who collapsed to the floor like an empty suit. The girl scurried backward, crouching against a wall, her head darting back and forth. She continued chewing on the bloody flesh. The bleeding man lay on the floor, too weak to move.

Kyle stared at her once-green eyes, now dilated into black spheres. Her mascara slowly melted down her cheeks.

"Hey there," he said, inching his way toward her. "It's okay. I'm not gonna hurt you."

Above her blood-spattered mouth and chin, the girl's forehead glistened with sweat, her pale, freckled skin now red with fever. Like a cornered animal, she snarled at Kyle. Crystal pounded on the window, her muffled voice pleading, "Kyle, are you crazy? Get out!"

Walters motioned for Crystal to be quiet. He grinned, mumbling, "I know what I'm doing."

"What's your name?" he politely asked.

But the girl said nothing. Instead she just growled. Kyle persisted, repeating his question.

"What's your na—"

"K-Ki-i-i-m. Her name is Kim."

Kyle looked at the dying man, his head barely lifted while his deep neck wound ebbed his life away. He struggled to form words amid the gurgling noises bubbling from his throat.

"S-s-she's my daughter," he said, choking. And with that his head hit the floor with a dull thud. He perished on that department store floor, encircled by a pool of his own blood.

The girl saw this and unveiled a red-toothed smile, licking her lips. The zombie virus was raging uncontrollably inside her, growing stronger by the minute.

Walters pressed on. "Kim, I'm Kyle, and I'm here to help you. Just take my hand and come with me. I can make you better. Trust me."

Kyle was defying everything he knew to be true by promising her that. It was just like him to take a risk. To tempt fate. To flirt with death. That was his style. His overconfidence was kicking into overdrive. He'd cheated death so many times before as a daredevil. Only now he was daring a real devil.

But to Kyle, the young redhead was more than just a typical soon-to-be zombie. He knew her name and that she had a loving dad who had taken his daughter shopping. She was a person, not a killer, and he was determined to rescue her from the demon disease inside.

Sirens blared in the distance as Kyle now stood directly in front of the girl.

"Kim, you and I are gonna walk out of here, together. I *promise* no one will hurt you."

The teenager slowly lifted her face, and Kyle saw the shiny, new pendant hanging around her neck. At the end of a thin, gold chain was the number 16.

"Happy birthday, Kim," he said softly, smiling.

Kyle thought he saw the green returning to her eyes, and this gave him hope . . . which further fed his confidence. She timidly placed her bloodstained hand in his and returned the smile, only this time it revealed gratitude, not lustful hunger.

"Let's go," he said.

The two of them started toward the doors, stepping over the dead man's body along the way. The police were outside with guns drawn and crouching behind the safety of their open cruiser doors. Shuffling her feet, the girl walked hand in hand with Kyle, finally reaching the exit.

Then she abruptly stopped and gripped Kyle's arm, locking down on it like a vise. Walters had never felt such strength before, especially from a female. He winced in pain and looked at her, confused. Her body contorted, causing her long nails to penetrate his jacket into his forearm.

"DON'T!" he pleaded. "We're almost there. I promise, no one is going to hurt—"

A deep, ghoulish groan exited the girl's throat. Her last ounce of decency was now strangled to death by the virus in charge. Like a cobra, she struck at Kyle's bicep, clenching her teeth around it and ripping it off with one bite. She jerked her head back, sending fabric and flesh sliding across the floor.

Crystal unleashed a bone-chilling shriek. The crowd gasped in unison. Ben stood paralyzed with fear. And Kyle fell into a sitting position on the department store floor, his mouth open, his right arm barely hanging by a few tendons. No one had to tell him. He knew he was dying from a massive loss of blood. And yet he felt no regret for what he had done. Instead, Kyle Walters felt like he understood what it meant to be *like* her.

But he didn't know why.

With what remained of his life spurting out of him, Kyle moistened his mouth and swallowed, then closed his eyes and slowly fell back onto the hard tile floor.

Chapter 9

THE UNHOLY ALLIANCE

There is no neutral ground in the universe; every square inch, every split second, is claimed by God and counter-claimed by Satan.

—C. S. Lewis

An Invisible Kingdom

There's something in the air. A scent. An ambience. It's not something you detect with your physical sense of smell at all. It's something else. An invisible stench in the space we occupy. Pungent and permeating our culture, homes, and lives, this foul odor is everywhere. We all inhale and exhale it, subconsciously and constantly. Every day. It lives in the realm of the spiritual, and only those who are spiritual can detect it. Some have a greater sense of smell than others. Like the family dog, whose sensory organs are some one hundred times that of its owner, some Christians have a greater natural or trained sensitivity to the spiritual world. These people are able to discern and "sniff out" what's in the air, enabling them to detect the enemy.

You knew you had an enemy, right?

He was once a holy angel. But fueled by an inner pride, this high-ranking, special cherub chose to rebel against the sovereign God. We spoke of him earlier. But since his famous Garden deception scheme, he's been very busy. His name—Satan—means "Adversary," and he is a notorious soul criminal. But he is also known by other aliases, among them:

- the "accuser of our brothers" (Revelation 12:10)
- Apollyon (or "Destroyer") (Revelation 9:11)
- the devil (Matthew 4:1)
- the dragon (Revelation 12:7)
- the father of lies (John 8:44)
- Lucifer, son of the morning (Isaiah 14:12 KJV)
- murderer (John 8:44)
- that old serpent (Revelation 12:9; 20:2 KJV)
- the prince of this world (John 12:31; 14:30; 16:11)
- prince of the power of the air (Ephesians 2:2 KJV)
- a roaring lion (1 Peter 5:8)
- a ruler of darkness (Ephesians 6:12)
- the tempter (Matthew 4:3; 1 Thessalonians 3:5)
- the thief (John 10:10)
- the evil one (wicked one, in KJV) (Matthew 13:19, 38)
- the enemy (Matthew 13:39)

This spiritual villain is the ultimate bad guy. And he hates you. *Really* hates you. He can't stand the sight of you. It's difficult to comprehend the concept of pure, undiluted hate. This commander of demons detests you so much that he wants to devour you like a lion does its prey![1] And that is not a pretty sight or a pleasant experience for the prey. He is aware that if you really want to hurt a father, you hurt his children. Doing this will touch the most tender part of a daddy's heart. And therein lies Satan's motivation. To vent his hatred for God by getting to his children. Though he played a part in the death of Christ, his rifle scope is now set on *you*.[2] Satan can't be in more than one place at once, and maybe it's a little presumptuous to think that you're so important that he would personally focus his attack on you. However, though they are finite beings, angels and demons are not limited by time or space as we are. That means they have the ability to travel instantaneously from one location to another. Consider also that Satan has command over a vast army of dark spirits, each one commissioned with the task of enslaving humanity to sin. They're on a combat mission, and you are their target.

One of Satan's greatest strategies involves orchestrating the spirit of this age to work in concert with his awful plans for humanity. He is the "god of this world" (2 Corinthians 4:4 KJV) and the "prince of the power of the air" (Ephesians 2:2 KJV). In other words, you and I are immersed in a spiritual system of values and thought—written, produced, directed, and dominated by the devil himself.[3]

Satan is the literal ruler of a spiritual kingdom. And this spiritual world is as real as the one you and I see and touch each day. Even more so. Because he is a ruler, he has great power and authority, with the ability to command his demonic troops, yet not without God's permission (Job 1:6–12; Luke 22:31–32). Psalm 24:1 tells us that the earth and everything in it belongs to the Lord. But for reasons known only to him, he's allowed the devil access to humanity and the planet we inhabit. So what's the devil up to?

Free Food

His first objective is to blind your eyes with deceptions and distractions. Because he's had thousands of years to observe and interact with humanity, he understands us intricately. He knows how we think, what our basic weaknesses are. He plays to our insecurities and fears. He caresses our sin nature. He feeds the zombie within.

But this evil genius has also taken this war against you a step further by creating a network of thought (which Scripture calls "the world"). It's a mind filter through which we perceive and interpret life, reality, relationships, and morality. This filter distorts our views concerning sex, personal freedoms, money, authority, decision making, family, parenting, dating, time management, cultural values, personal responsibility, and even theology. And each distortion is an anti-God narcotic, cooked up to feed our addiction to self.

Imagine the world this way. Your zombie roams the invisible streets of society, and on every corner is a "brain café" where the food is mostly free. The Internet is full of brains. The media is a brain buffet. Brains at school. Brains at work. Brains on TV. Brains on your iPhone. Brains in the locker room. Brains at your friend's house. Brains in the dorm room. Brains in the classroom. Brains, brains, *brains!* There is no shortage of brains for your zombie. And you don't even have to go looking for them. Brains are marketed to you every day. Constantly spammed to you through life itself. Just *being here* wins you a spot at the living-dead dinner table. Zombie food is in plentiful supply, and it always will be. There will never be a famine or a shortage. Satan is the master chef, and you are a perpetually starving customer. The world is his turf, and you're walking on it.

Because he is influencing thought throughout humanity, this would explain why media, advertising, music, government, law, science, philosophy, and education—either passively or proactively—propagate ungodly values. This of course doesn't mean that every one of them is totally dominated by worldly philosophies. But in case you have any doubt, just compare the values bred and spread in today's pop culture with those found in your Bible. Though at times there may be some accidental overlap, the majority are in stark contrast with Scripture and its God.

Satan has poisoned our water at the source. It flows freely into every home. And you and I drink from its tap every day. As lovers of God, we would instinctively want to run from this contamination, isolating ourselves from these influences. And yet God doesn't call us to do that. In place of isolation, he instead recommends *insulation*. In other words, he wants us to remain in the world, surrounded by the dark thought that permeates our atmosphere. Jesus put it this way in the prayer he offered to his Father the night before he died: "My prayer is not that you take them out of the world but that you protect them from the evil one. They are not of the world, even as I am not of it. Sanctify them by the truth; your word is truth. As you sent me into the world, I have sent them into the world."[4]

If God wanted us removed from the world, he'd just take us to heaven the moment we trusted in Christ. So there must be a purpose for us being left down here. In this same prayer, Jesus reminded the Father that his disciples' identity is not derived from the things of this world. How we view ourselves is not determined by the times in which we live or by what culture says we should be or do. Our identity is *in Christ*. This Earth hotel is not our home. We are only visiting this planet. We are aliens and strangers.[5] That's why God clearly calls us to set our minds on "things above," not on earthly things.[6]

A Trilogy of Temptation

So just how does Satan use the world to entice and arouse our inner beasts? We get a clue from the apostle John: "Do not love the world nor the things in the world. If anyone loves the world, the love of the Father is not in him. For all that is in the world, the lust of the flesh and the lust of the eyes and the boastful pride of life, is not from the Father, but is from the world. The world is passing away, and also its lusts; but the one who does the will of God lives forever."[7]

John was telling us that affection for God and affection for worldly values are mutually exclusive. They don't mix. They do not coexist. They are not friends.[8] It is impossible to both love God and be romantically involved with the spirit of this age. You will always gravitate toward one over the other. The greater your love for one, the less your love and loyalty will be for the other, until eventually, devotion to one cancels out devotion to the other. Love for the world is the only love God hates. And what is "out there" in the world that appeals to the flesh junkies living inside of us?

In a word, *lust.* The lust of the flesh. The lust of the eyes. The word means "strong desire," and can be directed toward something good—or not so good. The "lust of the flesh" refers to our unrighteous physical wants and cravings—everything from excessive food to ungodly friends to illicit sex. The flesh lusts a lot. The lust of the eyes is the craving for things. Stuff. It is, simply, materialism, an inordinate desire for possessions and anything else that is pleasant to the eyes (remember Genesis 3:6?). This isn't referring to a healthy desire and admiration for beauty, as in nature, art, or humanity. There is nothing wrong with admiring a beautiful girl or a handsome man (or an awesome car, for that matter). It's when that admiration turns to lust that we have a problem. This lust is often related to wanting what other people have, something Jesus warned us about.[9]

The pride of life is the third in this trilogy of temptation and signifies an obsession with self and self-importance. It's a preoccupation with impressing other people and perfectly plays right into our natural insecurity. This one is a hidden trap. Most of us would rather die than lose our social standing. Zombie pride at its best.

Interestingly, these were the same three areas Satan used to tempt Jesus while he was fasting in the desert (Matthew 4:1–11).

The Bible doesn't say the world *creates* these lustful temptations, but rather that they *exist* in the world. They are here because people are in the world. People with lust-monsters living inside them. Our naturally sinful desires are aroused and enticed by what we find in the world. We are susceptible to a personal love affair with a world ideology masterminded by one whose obsessive desire is to lie, deceive, steal, kill, and destroy.[10]

Satan and his dark spirit conspirators strategically set traps for us based on our weaknesses and previous behavior. But there is also a general aspect as well, as if culture casts a broad net to see how many human fish it can catch. Two very effective methods of enslaving the ones God loves. In this way the world and Satan partner with the walking dead inside us. And make no mistake about sin. It is never the devil's fault. Or the world's. Sin happens because we *want* it to, as our Lord's half brother noted.[11]

Hmm. So *we* are ultimately responsible for giving in to temptation. That's not nearly as fun as blaming the devil or the big, bad world.

Human Clay

So that's how Satan and his system work you from the inside. But he doesn't stop there. Remember, his goal is total domination and destruction of you. Consequently, he has another battle plan, uncovered by Paul, who warned us, "Do not conform . . . to the pattern of this world, but be transformed by the renewing of your mind."[12]

This phrase "conform to the pattern of this world" pictures being pressed like putty or clay into a mold. As we've said, this age, or "world," is characterized by a system of beliefs and values contrary to God's. Ours is not a morally neutral culture. And these beliefs and values don't stand still. Instead, they circulate like information on the Internet—constantly and at the speed of thought. And we cannot navigate this matrix alone. The age in which we live is both a torrent and a tyrant, and the pressure to conform is enormous. We're not talking about surface issues, like clothing or music styles. It's more a way of looking at life. It's the lens through which you see everything, including yourself. And there are only two kinds of lenses— God's and the world's.

The antidote to this worldly venom? A "mind revolution," Paul said. Or in biblical language, being "transformed by the renewing of your mind." Instead of having your brain devoured by the zombie inside you, allow God to transform the way you think. Let him flush out your old way of thinking about things and replace it with his thoughts. Doing this "renews" your mind, rebooting it to start fresh. One of the reasons we make some of the dumbest choices in our lives is because we've allowed the values of this age to infiltrate our thinking. So when it comes time to make decisions—about friendships, relationships, marriage, career, money, or sex—our brains are already filled with worldly "wisdom." This thinking affects our emotions in those areas as well. And we wonder why our lives are so messed up.[13] But here's the exciting part: if we feed God's thoughts to our souls (found in his Word), we breathe new life into our minds and are able to navigate life with much more confidence and clarity. A mind revolution.

But you and I are getting played from both ends—the world

on the outside and the sin nature on the inside. The unholy alliance. They have a common goal—to enslave us to ungodly thinking, sin, and addiction to self. And if possible, our total annihilation.

Then how do we fight this Satan? Well, we could start by not being stupid. Realize that he has an evil ally and a spy living inside you. Don't be ignorant of who your enemy is and what his tactics are in your personal life. Be alert and aware.[14] Get fitted for battle, because we're in a war here.[15] The bullets are real, and people die every day from this conflict. There are surprise attacks, snipers perched in high places, and explosives deliberately and cleverly hidden on your path. It's dirty warfare. And you won't live a day in this life when you are not attacked in some way. The enemy has a mission, and he will do whatever it takes. There are no rules of engagement in this war. Satan is a terrorist and has declared an unholy war against you.

Like it or not, you're in training for the ZTF.

Episode Ten

CONSPIRACY THEORY

The raging redhead resumed feasting on Kyle's arm, but was distracted by the scent of more flesh outside. Leaving the two dead men at her feet, she staggered through the department store doors toward the crowd. Four shots rang out, and she was dead before hitting the ground. A six-person disease control unit hurriedly placed the three bodies into thick plastic bags and sped away before the corpses could reanimate. Kyle's body was the last to be bagged, and Ben caught a final glimpse of his friend as the long zipper passed over his face. The police then took an on-site statement before allowing the couple to leave the scene. Everything was pretty routine for this sort of thing, if you can call two people having their flesh ripped apart by a high school girl "routine."

The display on the bank across the street flashed the temperature. It was forty-five degrees. Having been overcast all day long, it now started to rain. Ben and Crystal scurried to the car, and once inside, Ben made the awkward phone call to Rick to tell him what had happened.

Driving back to his warehouse office, neither of them said a word. Crystal put her head on Ben's shoulder, weeping silently as he drove. The rain was coming down harder now, sending Ben into an even darker, more pensive mood. He tried to make some sense of what had just happened. He wanted to know *why.* A barrage of questions bombarded his mind: *Why did I go downtown today? Why did I run into Kyle? If I had left thirty minutes earlier . . . if Crystal hadn't seen that handbag . . .* It was a circular thought process leading nowhere. A mind game. And this brought him no comfort.

Dan would say it was simply Kyle's "time." "And when it's your time, no force known to man can prevent it," he'd once said. This reasoning was partially what helped Dan cope with his dad's death. In reality, it was a philosophical Band-Aid placed on a deep emotional wound.

Ben was hypnotized by the rhythmic cadence of the windshield wipers, his thoughts alternating back and forth in sync with them. *Does this mean I'm next?* he wondered.

"Prepared and protected, boys," his dad always said whenever they went camping or hiking.

You were prepared for everything, Dad. Except the one time you really needed to be. But how can I ever prepare myself for days like today? Ben asked himself silently, wishing for an answer.

Pulling into the parking garage near Sk8X, the couple ran hand in hand through the rain and into the building. Sonya was waiting. She'd clearly been crying, and upon seeing Ben, she ran around the desk, giving him a long hug.

"Thank God. I'm so glad you're okay."

"We're fine. Just . . . just kinda freaked-out," Ben replied, returning the embrace.

Sonya wiped her eyes. "Everybody's in the conference room. We should go on in now. You too, Crystal."

The three walked in and took their seats at the large oak table. Ben and Crystal were soaked from the rain, which continued outside.

"Guys, I don't even know where to begin," Rick confessed. "And I don't have any answers. On a day like today, publishing a magazine doesn't matter much in the grand scheme of things. However, it might do us some good to hear what exactly happened. That is, Ben, if you feel up to it."

Ben actually *didn't* feel up to it. All he really wanted was to run away. To be anywhere he could be free from the threat of blood-fueled zombie attacks. Just somewhere alone would be a great start. He felt haunted.

He ran his jacket sleeve across his forehead, absorbing a gathering puddle of rainwater just above his dark eyebrows. Ben related the incident to his coworkers as they stared at him in shock and disbelief.

Crystal gave her boyfriend's hand a reassuring squeeze under the table.

And that was it. The Sk8X staff got up and left, each of them wearing a pale look of death. Sonya took Crystal to the ladies' room to help put her back together. Left alone and shivering in his wet clothes, Ben got up to go see if he might find an old Sk8X T-shirt in the storage room. After flipping the light switch, he rummaged through several boxes before locating a lone, white T-shirt. Upon peeling off his drenched top, he slipped on the dry shirt and instantly felt better. From the confines of the room, Ben heard the thunder reverberate through the brick walls as the rain incessantly pelted the roof over his head.

Reclining on a pallet of magazines, Ben ran a hand through his wet hair and wondered how many times Kyle had napped right where he was sitting. "Nobody like Walters," he mumbled.

Then he spotted something on the floor beside him.

Reaching down, he discovered it to be a well-worn paperback with frayed edges. Ben flipped the book over, reading the title out loud: *"Covert Cure: Our Government's Cover-Up of the Z-38 Antidote,* by Dr. Donald Cumberland." The back bio read:

Dr. Donald Cumberland, PhD, is a renowned forensic pathologist and infamous whistleblower on the "Arms for Uranium Deal." A former Marine, Dr. Cumberland has spent the better part of his life solving mysteries and bringing secrets to light. In 1998, he was awarded the prestigious "Beacon of Light" prize by the Association for Government Accountability. Dr. Cumberland used the grant from this award to found the Center for Integrity, a Washington, D.C., think tank investigative group.

"Walters, you were such a nut." But with nothing else to do and needing some distraction, Ben opened the book and casually began reading.

In the introduction, Cumberland claimed to have uncovered credible information suggesting that some twenty years ago our government discovered an antivirus that halted the spread of Z-38 from stage 1 to stage 2, and in some tests even *reversed* the effects of stage 3. In other words, a near-complete cure for the zombie virus!

"That," Cumberland wrote, "means our government has possessed the ability to eradicate the world's deadliest disease for some two decades and has done nothing about it! In the pages to follow, you will learn how this cure was found, who knows about it, and most important, why it's been kept top-secret."

Dr. Cumberland sounded like a man with a flair for the dramatic, and Ben's curiosity was aroused. The premise definitely sounded like a great movie plot. But was it the *truth*? That would require a lot more persuasion. So while the rain poured outside, Ben leaned against the brick wall of the storage room and turned the page.

The author claimed that in the winter of 2002, he discovered an envelope wedged inside the back door of his Arlington, Virginia, home. Opening it, he found a picture of a smiling little girl, along with a hand-scribbled note that read: "The entire world can have this kind of joy. If you want to know more, meet me tonight. Arlington Cemetery, Tomb of the Unknown Soldier, 6 p.m. Come alone and tell no one about this." The note was unsigned.

Dr. Cumberland explained:

Half of me thought this person was a full-fledged crack-pot, and I wondered if I would be the victim of some sort of elaborate ruse. But the other half of me, the scientist within, longed to know more. So I followed my investigative instincts.

It was a bitterly cold day in our nation's capital. A light snow had begun to fall. Arriving that evening, 6 p.m. on the dot, I spotted a lone figure on the observation steps across from the Tomb. I approached him cautiously and quietly hoped that if he should assault me in some way, the Sentinel marching nearby might rush to my rescue. My fears, however, proved to be unfounded, as the man on the steps turned out to be a small fellow. He wore a beard and was dressed in a long, black coat, with a dark fedora covering his head. A sprinkle of snow lightly decorated his shoulders and the encircling brim of his hat. This man extended a gloved hand, introducing himself only as "Mr. Brown." We retreated to the covering of a nearby portico, and our covert conversation began.

"Dr. Cumberland, thank you for meeting me. What I am about to tell you is highly classified information. The implications of this intel carry catastrophic consequences. And my very life could be in jeopardy. Officially, I am not here, and this conversation never happened."

I nodded, indicating I understood, and he continued.

"In 1992, I was working in the State Department, in a division of the National Security Agency, when I stumbled upon a memo sent to my superior from the vice president. According to the memo, then president James Mitchell had just been made aware of a research breakthrough by the Centers for Disease Control. A privately owned jet was sent to Atlanta, and the director of the CDC was brought directly to the White House. Once inside the Oval Office, he excitedly presented his center's findings to the president. Present in the Oval Office that day were the president, the vice president, the president's chief of staff, and national security adviser Bert Scallett. According to the memo, the announcement was greeted with muted enthusiasm. The CDC director was thanked for his diligent work and then abruptly flown back to Atlanta under strict orders to tell no one of this until hearing from the president.

"Bear in mind that just twenty-four months earlier, President Mitchell was elected on a campaign platform to unite the world's superpowers around a cohesive effort to find a cure for Z-38. To his credit, he founded and chaired the first-ever global summit on 'Tomorrow's Hope,' his term describing a zombie-free planet. This prominent international role would be strategic in his reelection campaign and place in history."

The snow continued to fall as Mr. Brown elaborated.

"Now consider, Dr. Cumberland, the dilemma facing this president: he was sitting atop the greatest discovery in human history. He now had more power than any ten of his predecessors combined, possessing the authority to end the most horrific plague ever to threaten mankind. But the phone in the CDC director's office never rang. For back at the White House, the president—along with his top advisors—convened long into the night, debating the dilemma. And in a unanimous decision, it was concluded that they should not release the news of this breakthrough cure to the public.

"But why not? Why not just release the cure and take credit for it? Consider their reasoning: First, acknowledging a cure would plunge the U.S. economy into immediate collapse. Keep in mind, multiple government agencies, research facilities, hundreds of treatment centers, border protection, and one-third of the CDC all exist solely because of the threat of Z-38. One hundred percent of their funding depends on it. No more zombies means no more money for these agencies. And ninety-three thousand people are suddenly unemployed. No sitting president wants *that* job loss as a stain on his résumé and legacy. Second, about a fourth of all state and federal taxes levied went toward funding research and containment of the living dead. A cure meant this government gravy train would suddenly derail. In addition, some nineteen nations have similar organizations, all dependent on "zombie-funds" from the United States. Releasing the cure would impact the global economy, weakening other countries' indebtedness to and dependence on us.

"So, Dr. Cumberland, you can understand why this has been a well-guarded secret. Only a small circle of people in each new administration are brought into the loop. Unofficially, they call themselves '*Les Guardiens*,' or 'the Guardians.' Each of these top administration officials, including the president, is sworn to a seventy-five-year oath of silence. My sources inform me that in return for their silence, these people receive regular antivirus vaccinations for life. A fitting reward in exchange for a lifetime of silence, wouldn't you say? That is, if you can handle the guilt associated with sending countless innocent people to their deaths each day.

"Our government is saving the release of this cure for a rainy day, that, of course, being a major zombie outbreak. This is the ultimate ace of spades up the sleeve of every U.S. president. Should a zombie outbreak occur during his term in office, he can ride in, as it were, on a white horse, with cure in hand, saving the day. And they won't be able to sandblast his face on Mount Rushmore fast enough. The past three presidents have held that card, yet destiny has not selected them to play it.

"Lastly, imagine the wrath of the American people upon learning that a cure for Z-38 has been available since 1992. Imagine the trillions of dollars in lawsuits resulting from family members whose relatives have perished from this zombie scourge. Not to mention the outrage, protests, rioting in the streets, looting, marching on the White House . . . perhaps even a violent overthrow of our government. It would be an irreparable tear in our national fabric, perhaps even the end of our society. And this president knows it. We could not survive the scandal and potential revolution. And now, we are way too long into the great lie, and much too deep into the rabbit hole to turn back.

"It comes down to *money* . . . and the preservation of our very way of life. Should you desire to investigate further, I suggest you begin by locating whom you deem to be the weakest cabinet member of our past three administrations. Find out who has nothing to lose by talking. This person is the open window into this house of horrors. This is all I can say. And I remind you once again, this conversation never happened."

Continuing, Cumberland wrote:

The plummeting temperature, combined with the chill-
ing thought of such a thing being true gave me a shiver.
The dark figure shook my hand and bade me farewell, disappearing into the night through a thick curtain of snow.
And though I now had enough ammunition to bring the
government to its knees, I nevertheless had to verify his
unbelievable story. And that's what I've been doing these
past seven years: researching, documenting, interviewing
witnesses, and tracking down leads. So convinced was I
that I liquidated my life savings, retired from my medical
practice, and pursued this earth-shattering revelation. That
clandestine winter's eve rendezvous forever changed my
life. I've chosen to break this story to the world because of
an unfailing principle that has guided me since childhood:
Verum in vita. Supremus totus. Translated from Latin, it
means "Truth in life. Above all."

Ben finished *Covert Cure* in three hours.

If all this is true, he thought, *it makes the JFK assassination conspiracy seem like solving a crossword puzzle. On the
other hand, if Cumberland made up the whole thing, including
"Mr. Brown," then he's just another guy looking to make a buck.*

● ● ●

An hour later, Sonya and Crystal walked into the storeroom
and found Ben asleep on a pallet of magazines, a tattered
paperback resting on his chest.

It was still raining outside.

Chapter 10

NIGHTMARE OF THE LIVING DEAD

Above all the grace and the gifts that Christ gives to his beloved is that of overcoming self.
—**St. Francis of Assisi**

Laws of Nature

Sir Isaac Newton was a brilliant seventeenth-century mathematician and physicist. You may remember him as the guy who discovered gravity when an apple fell on his head. And while that particular story may be fictional, Sir Isaac did introduce the idea to the world. But that wasn't all he gave us. Besides his famous law of gravity, he also discovered something called the law of universal gravitation. This law states that the mass of two objects and the distance between them control the force of gravity between the two. If two objects possess great mass, the force will be greater. And if the objects are close, the force will be even greater. For example, if the moon were the size of the earth, then assuming it remained in its current orbit, it would soon collide with our planet, giving new meaning to the expression "I got mooned."

Since you struggle with sin, you understand the frustration that accompanies this uncivil war within. You're aware of the gravitational pull of your sin nature. It's a spiritual mass, not something physical that you can touch. But it's just as real. This downward pull is a spiritual law reflecting a physical law. The things we see with our physical eyes are temporary, but the unseen world is eternal. And in this realm, spiritual gravitational forces keep us earthbound, preventing us from escaping its bonds. But in the world of physics, there is an even greater force than gravity. It's called magnetic force, and you've seen it at work in ordinary magnets. One magnet can lift another off a table, thus defying the weaker law of gravity. Their attraction to each other makes them virtually inseparable.

This magnetic force illustrates the fatal attraction going on between the two yous. A powerful pull toward each other. Sometimes it's subtle. Sometimes overt. But nevertheless present at all times. It's undeniable and seemingly unconquerable. And the inward battle weakens us to the point that we end up doing the very things we hate. Crazy, huh? We know it's wrong, but we do it anyway, don't we? And why? Because it feels so good to feed the beast.

This war stems from a spiritual genetic code we inherited from Adam. Creation's first man became a sinner by sinning. We, on the other hand, sin *because* we are sinners. The root determines the fruit. That dungeon desire within seems almost primal at times, like a prehistoric seed of wickedness. This ancient evil is embedded inside us. A simmering cauldron of vice, begging to be released. And so you grant the request. Circumstances of life can pry open that door to hell within us. For example, your day goes wrong. A relationship turns sour. Emotions rise and then go unchecked, and before you know it, you're burning up in a fever of anger or spiraling into a depressive abyss. Or equally unhealthy, falling in love with a toxic person. It's all a part of the deception. The illusionist living somewhere between your soul and spirit creating an identity crisis.

The biggest fails of all occur when we: (1) underestimate the sin nature's power; (2) think we can peacefully coexist with it; and (3) believe that we somehow have it under control, or worse, that we've conquered it for good.

So what are we supposed to do about all of this? How do we survive, manage, and defeat the zombie living within? And is that even possible?

We've seen that becoming more religious isn't the answer. Trying harder, no matter how sincere you are, just won't cut it. We've also discovered that adding more Christian rules, standards, and restrictions can't change us on the inside. So what are we to do? The good news is that God has provided a solution for us, and it's one that works. But in order for us to experience a win here, we have to literally "reprogram" our minds. We think in patterns we have learned from past experience. We are so used to the same tired old solutions that our minds have trouble rethinking or reimagining a different way. And that's exactly why Paul encouraged us to be "transformed by the renewing of [our] mind[s]."[1]

Unplugged

The journey to victory begins with God's truth, and by encountering what he has done to free us from the magnetic lust-force within. It all started when you placed your trust in Jesus Christ for salvation. Whether as a small child or more recently, the moment you put your faith in Jesus, you were baptized by the Holy Spirit.[2] Now, depending on your church background, you may have a certain mental picture of the concept of baptism. But here Paul wasn't referring to being dunked under water or sprinkled by a pastor at the front of the church. Instead, he was speaking of spiritual baptism. In Paul's world, when garment makers wanted to turn white cloth into red cloth, they dipped the material into a vat of dye. Completely immersed underwater, the fabric would begin to absorb the color of the dye so that when it was lifted out of the vat, it would be red. The cloth was then fully *identified* with the color of the dye. The word they used to describe this process was *baptize*. Paul, tapping into his culture, used this word to describe what happens to us at salvation. The instant you trusted Christ, God's Spirit immersed (baptized) you into Christ, identifying you with him. So when you see the word *baptize* in Scripture, think *identify*. That's a spiritual truth, and a somewhat mystical concept that can be hard to sink our teeth into. But that's exactly why we have to retrain our minds to think this way. We are spiritual beings who have learned to rely way too much on our physical senses. We have to learn to think more spiritually.

Becoming a disciple of Jesus is, and has always been, about identifying yourself with him. And we sort of get that idea, but only with regard to how we're supposed to *live* for him. The *doing* part we get. But it's the *being* part that God wants us to grasp and wrap our minds around. We are not the same people we once were. We have been changed. Transformed. Reborn. We've each been given a new identity and a new nature.[3]

But wait, you may be thinking. *If I have a new nature, then why is the old nature still around?*

Great question. And once again, Paul comes to our rescue. He told the Roman believers they had been "baptized into Christ Jesus . . . buried with him through baptism . . . united with him," and because of this we're "freed from sin." He then added that the "old self was crucified with him."[4]

Paul had just explained to his readers that God's grace was so huge that the more mankind sinned, the bigger his grace got. But just in case we think we should keep sinning so that grace will cover us, he penned those words in Romans. First, he said we have "died to sin."[5] But in what sense is this true? The Bible always signifies death as separation, not extinction. When a person dies, he or she doesn't cease to exist. But that person's physical body is *separated* from his or her spirit.[6] And when a believer dies, the body goes into the ground, and the spirit goes to be with the Lord.[7] Separated. And one day to be reunited again.[8] But until that time comes, our bodies "groan," waiting for the day when we'll finally be free from sin.[9]

So in what sense did we "die to sin"? And how are we now "separated" from it? This freedom from sin, self, and Satan we now possess was purchased for us by Jesus through his death on the cross. As Jesus hung there, God the Father unleashed an eternal barrage of wrath onto his Son. The physical torment of the cross was miniscule compared to what was going on behind the scenes. God gathered up all of his righteous hatred and anger against sin and blasted Jesus with it for six hours. So intense was this torment that he treated Jesus as if he *were* sin itself.[10] An eternity of hell compacted into six hours' time. That's a brain bender, and I don't fully understand it. I also don't completely understand all of what hell is—only that it's a real place, populated by those who refused to trust in Jesus, and that it's eternal, involving unimaginable torment.[11] Those currently in hell experience what Jesus experienced on the cross, only it lasts for eternity. Can you even imagine that?

But a second aspect to Jesus' suffering on the cross was that the punishment for sin also included *death*. "The wages of sin is death" (Romans 6:23; emphasis added). In other words, we "earn" the penalty of death just by being sinners. The Bible says Jesus died "for our sins."[12] He took on that punishment. But beyond merely suffering the penalty of physical death, there was something else happening at the same time. Just having his heart stop wasn't the only death Jesus experienced. Remember Scripture's definition of death as "separation"? Sin separates us from God, preventing relationship and intimacy.[13] Part of the punishment Jesus suffered on our behalf was that the Father turned his back on him during that six-hour window. Jesus was abandoned. Left alone. Isolated. Cut off. Deserted. Forsaken. Left in utter loneliness. And not because of anything he had done. That total abandonment was reserved for you and me. But Jesus said, "Father, give it to me instead." So, on the cross, Jesus was disconnected from everything related to goodness and God—including love, peace, happiness, companionship, laughter, joy, fulfillment, and hope.

This double-barrel judgment of torment and isolation is precisely what Jesus went through while on the cross. But through his death, he rendered Satan powerless.[14] At the cross, the power of sin and self was voided, and God's proof of this was the resurrection. Because we are "in Christ,"[15] we have been identified with Jesus through spiritual baptism, and we are considered "dead to sin" through faith in him. In other words, sin, self, and Satan no longer have any legal right to ownership or control over us. They have all been "disconnected" from us. Unplugged. The power turned off. Rendered impotent. And in their place, the Spirit of God now resides in us, along with our new nature (2 Corinthians 5:17). The old nature still exists and will remain with us until we go to heaven. But its power, authority, control, and influence over us have been made obsolete. We don't have to obey its lusts any longer (Romans 6:12–14). We are free. Free to know God and be devoted to him.

Acknowledging this is part of transforming our minds to think differently about ourselves. We don't naturally think this way. Our minds are full of toxic thoughts and thought patterns. We are accustomed to believing the lie that Satan and self have sold to us for years: "It's just the way I am, and there's no use trying to change me."

But the truth is that you have been changed already! Your old self is dead (separated from you) and you are now "in Christ." And the life you now live, you live by faith in the One who gave himself to set you free from the beast inside.[16]

You and I are not bound or obligated to obey our inner zombies. And nothing in this universe can *make* us. We're genuinely *free*. That's really great news, isn't it?

The Strong Force

But back to the age-old question: "If I have been identified with Christ, and the old nature is crucified with him, why do I still sin every day?"

Keep in mind that though the old sin nature has been rendered powerless, it is still within you. Like the Z-38 virus, it can lie dormant. It's still a part of our humanity, and its potential for destruction is still exponential. God has graciously given us the gift of choice. Because we are in Christ, we have the ability to choose obedience, whereas before we were literally unable to do so.[17] So when you experience temptation from the flesh, you can now choose whether or not you will listen and give in to it. And that's a choice empowered by the Spirit who now lives within you. More about that later.

But here's the important thing about this choice we now have. It's a daily thing. While our identification with Jesus, spiritual baptism, and freedom from the flesh happened once and for all at salvation, following God and resting in our new identity is a choice we make each day. Make that *many times* a day. Someone has wisely said, "The trouble with life is that it's so . . . *daily*!" But the foundation upon which we build these daily choices rests on the unchanging truth about who God says we are. Our daily thinking has to be rooted and grounded in God's truth. Otherwise we're dead meat. Christ won a great victory through his death and resurrection. He separated us from the power of sin and self, and the Spirit identified us with him. Therefore we have a new identity. But it takes time to reprogram our minds to think biblically. And in order to keep from being consumed by sin from within, we have to flood our minds with Scripture, but not because we're "supposed to." We have to for survival. We have to trust biblical truth, God's heart on paper. Then, and only then, will we have a fighting chance at winning this lifelong battle.

There's one more law of physics you should know about, and one Sir Isaac Newton couldn't possibly have discovered in the seventeenth century. This one has been dubbed "the strong force." According to physicists, it's the strongest force in the universe—100 times stronger than the electromagnetic force and 10^{38} times stronger than gravity! And where would you expect to find this kind of power? Surprisingly, it's found in the nucleus of the atom. The atom is made up of protons and neutrons. Protons have a positive electric charge, while neutrons have no charge at all. But the big question haunting quantum physicists is this: Since positively charged protons naturally repel themselves, what is actually holding the nucleus of an atom together?

What they discovered was that a mysterious force (which they still don't really understand) keeps those protons together. If this mysterious force were removed from the atom's nucleus, a nuclear reaction would occur (that's how they make atom bombs). Take the "strong force" away, and chaos and global cataclysmic destruction will follow. Nothing in our universe would exist anymore. But as strong as this greatest force is, it is only effective within the nucleus of the atom. Its supernatural power to hold together becomes weaker with distance.

This unknown force is a secret of nature and is still being studied. Interestingly, two thousand years ago, Paul wrote that Jesus Christ predates the universe, and "in him all things *hold together*."[18]

If God ever decided to "let go," every proton in every atom of every molecule would suddenly separate—and the universe, the earth, and *you* would be no more.

What keeps you and me together (physically and spiritually) is the power of Jesus Christ. He is our Strong Force. The power we need for our weak minds. A personal God sustaining us—physically, emotionally, mentally, and spiritually. And to overcome the evil within you, you will have to rely on this God and his power. His truth must be your guiding light. Your anchor. Your rock. He can and will empower you in the midst of each day to slay the living dead within.

And for that reason, he is a zombie's worst nightmare.

Episode Eleven

THE OLD ONES

Ben, wake up!" Crystal yelled at her boyfriend.

"Huh? Whaa . . ." Ben's body jolted, sending the paperback on his chest flying across the room. "What time is it?" he said, squinting his eyes and attempting to sit up.

"It's five o'clock. Have you been in here all this time?" Sonya asked.

Ben yawned, stretching his arms skyward. "Um, yeah. I guess the rain put me in a trance. Where have you guys been?"

"We've been in the break room, drinking hot tea and talking. Girl talk, mainly. Stuff you wouldn't understand, amigo." Sonya gave Ben a wink.

"Oh, no doubt. I'm an idiot on the subject."

"You're not an idiot," Crystal assured him. "You're just a typical guy."

"So where is everybody?" Ben asked.

"Rick's in his office, but everybody else has gone," Sonya said.

"Nope," a deep voice said over Sonya's shoulder. "Rick's right here."

"Oh my gosh, Rick! You scared me!" Sonya blurted.

"Do I even want to know what y'all are doing in the storage room? Surely our back issues can't be that stimulating," Rick said with a laugh.

"You're such a comedian," Sonya retorted sarcastically.

Rick changed the subject. "By the way, I spoke to the police. They've contacted Kyle's family in San Diego. His body is being shipped to a facility there tonight."

"That was quick," Sonya commented.

"Not really. They don't keep bodies around following an attack."

Ben walked across the room, retrieving the paperback off the floor.

"Rick," Sonya said, "we should go to Kyle's apartment and pack up his things for the family."

"I'm sure they'd appreciate that," Rick agreed.

"I won't be able to make it," Ben chimed. "But when you pack his things, put this in." He handed Sonya the book.

As the four exited the windowless room, Ben took a final look around. "See ya later, Kyle." Then, flipping off the light switch, he went home.

● ● ●

The next few weeks at Sk8X were dull and largely unproductive. The team was unmotivated, and the spirit was dark. The sting of Kyle's death was still very real to them all.

Thanksgiving was less than a week away, and Ben was looking forward to some relaxing time at his mom's house. Dan would be coming, and his mom had invited Crystal to eat with them as well. But to both sons' surprise, Patricia Forman had also asked a gentleman friend to Thanksgiving dinner. Both boys were anxious to meet the man, and specifically to approve or disapprove of him. But Thanksgiving was still almost a week away.

That Saturday, Ben took Crystal for a drive in the Smoky Mountains. He needed a diversion, some way of escaping the recent drama that had marked him the past few weeks. About forty-five minutes southwest of Corazon City is a place called Braxton's Tunnel, and Ben used to come here with his friends back in high school. The tunnel got its name from famed Confederate general Braxton Bragg, a North Carolina native known for his tenacious spirit and disciplined command. During the Civil War, the general oversaw the construction of a railroad from Charleston to Knoxville. It was a costly, labor-intensive, and time-sensitive effort, as Southern soldiers were in dire need of food, weapons, and reinforcements. But upon crossing the North Carolina border, engineers encountered an unexpected obstacle. A granite mountain. So Bragg developed a plan to bore straight through the massive rock. Fifteen hundred laborers blasted and hammered, their only tools being sledgehammers, pickaxes, and black powder. This project took much longer than anticipated. Finally, with just ninety feet to go, the South surrendered and the Civil War abruptly ended, prompting the men to drop their tools and head home. The tunnel was never completed.

Today, what's left of Braxton's Tunnel (also known as "Bragg's Folly") is a 30-foot-wide-by-25-foot-high abandoned hole bored some 1,637 feet deep into the mountain. Once past the entrance, pitch blackness takes over. It's so dark you can't see your hand in front of your face. Adding to the creepiness is a constant, tomb-cool temperature of fifty-six degrees. It's a longtime tradition for locals to journey the entire distance into the tunnel without candle or flashlight. For decades, explorers, thrill-seekers, and mischievous teenagers have made the long walk—only to discover that their fear of the dark was much greater than anticipated. Ben hadn't been there since high school.

After pulling into the gravel parking lot, Ben slipped a large flashlight into his coat pocket, and he and Crystal walked the few dozen yards through the woods leading to the tunnel's entrance.

Once near, Crystal hesitated, grabbing her boyfriend's hand. "Ben, wait. Are we sure we want to do this?"

"Are you kidding? We didn't drive all the way out here for nothing."

"But it's so dark in there."

"Duh, Crystal. That's the point, isn't it? Don't worry; it'll be fun. Look, I brought a flashlight in case you get scared. See?"

"Okay, but promise you won't leave me in there."

"Ha-ha. Yes, I promise."

"Ben, I'm serious. If you walk one foot away from me, I will kick your butt and never trust you again."

"Okay, okay. I swear I won't leave you. We'll hold hands the whole way. Deal?"

"Deal."

The couple passed the tunnel's huge entrance, and Ben let out a yell, hoping for an echo. Within a minute, the sun's natural light disappeared, and they were enveloped by blackness.

Ben whispered, "They say a lot of men died making this tunnel. Landslides and stuff. They also say people have disappeared in here over the years. Vagrants. Hikers. Runaways. Even couples."

"Hey, if you're trying to frighten me, mission accomplished, okay?"

Crystal turned to look back at the entrance of the tunnel, which was rapidly shrinking into a small, bright opening. She let go of Ben's hand, interlocking her arm with his.

"This is creeping me out. My eyes are wide-open, but I can't see a thing."

"Funny thing about the dark," he replied sarcastically. "Just hang on tight, all right?"

"That won't be a problem," Crystal assured him.

Ben shined the flashlight into the distant darkness. The light dissipated into nothingness.

"This thing is, like, five football fields long."

The couple continued their cautious journey into the deep mountain cave, the silence broken only by the sound of their reverberating footsteps and the accidental random kicking of small rocks.

"Know what I was just thinking?" Crystal said.

"Nope. I left my mind-reading device back in the car." Ben laughed.

She playfully slapped him on the chest. "You're not so funny, Ben Forman. Anyway, I was thinking about how I've never really been in the dark with you . . . like this. I think it's sort of . . . romantic, don't you?"

"Romantic?" Ben inquired.

"Yes, dummy. Romantic. You know, like between a guy and a girl who like each other? Do I have to spell it out for you?"

"No, that's okay. I think I get your meaning."

They continued their slow walk into the velvet hole, their eyes straining but seeing nothing. After another few minutes of silence, Crystal spoke again.

"So . . ."

"So . . . what?" Ben responded innocently.

"Are you that clueless? Come on. Here we are. Alone. Two people who like each other. Are you from another planet? Do you have a pulse? I want you to kiss me, silly."

"Now, how would I kiss you *silly*?"

"BEN!"

"I'm kidding." He laughed.

"What's your problem? You don't think I'm worth kissing

or something? 'Cause you've only kissed me once in, like, seven months, in case you don't remember."

"Hey, don't get upset. It's just that . . . um . . . the tradition at Braxton's Tunnel is to wait till you're all the way to the back wall before kissing. It's considered good luck. Don't worry; we're almost there . . . I think."

"Hmm. Okay, I'll wait," she reluctantly agreed.

They finally arrived at the tunnel's end. Ben shined his flashlight around, revealing the marks of pickaxes, still visible a century and a half later. Broken glass, bottles, and cans littered the cold, damp floor. And the silence was like nothing either of them had ever experienced. Ben shut off the flashlight.

"Sooo . . . ?" Crystal spoke up, reminding him.

"Oh yeah . . . the *tradition*. Um, okay. First you have to close your eyes."

"Hey, Einstein, you think it really matters in here?" Crystal laughed.

"Oh yeah, good point. Now, put your hands behind your back and count to five."

"What? Why?"

"Just do it."

"Aghhhh! Ben, you're so frustrating sometimes. Okay, my hands are behind my back . . . One . . . two . . . three . . . four . . . five . . . Um, I'm waiting . . . Ben? . . . BEN! Hello? Ben, PLEASE! Where are you . . . ?

"BOO!" he shouted, grabbing her waist from behind.

Crystal let out her trademark scream, causing Ben to laugh. "I got you. I *sooo* got you!"

"You scared the you-know-what outta me is what you did!"

"Hey, come here," said Ben, putting his arms around her. He hugged her tight, then kissed her lips softly.

It was a long kiss.

"See? That was worth the wait, wasn't it?"

"I don't know," Crystal protested. "It certainly wasn't worth the scare you gave me. I may need another one just to make sure."

Ben obliged his girlfriend, planting another soft kiss on her lips. He knew she liked that he made kissing her a special thing. Then, abruptly, Crystal produced a digital camera from her jacket and held it out blindly in front of them. The sudden brightness of the flash stung their eyes, having grown accustomed to the dark.

"Wow, oookay. That was unexpected," Ben said. "Hey, I think we should head out. It'll be almost dark by the time we reach the entrance."

The couple started toward the tunnel's opening.

"I'm glad we did this, Ben. It was fun. Definitely different—kinda creepy—but fun," Crystal said, grabbing his hand again.

"Me too. Like I said, I haven't been up here since high school. I remember this one time me and Jack Wilson—"

"Wait. What was that?" Crystal whispered.

"Shhhh! I heard it too. Sounded like a scream. Probably just a rat." Ben shined his flashlight but saw nothing. "Hello?" His flashlight's beam once again dissipated into the darkness ahead. "Let's just keep going, okay?"

Crystal concurred. "The sooner we get out of here, the better."

The pair walked faster now, feeling more claustrophobic. When they were almost halfway out, they heard the noise again.

"Hey, up there! Are you okay?" Ben shouted.

"Just keep going!" Crystal urged.

They picked up the pace, finally reaching the point where they could see light.

"See? We're almost there," Ben assured her.

The light also brought a long-awaited breath of fresh

outside air. In the distance he could see the waning afternoon sun's rays reflecting off of the orange mountain leaves. They started jogging toward the entrance. Then Ben suddenly stopped, grabbing Crystal around the waist.

"Hold up," he cautioned her.

Though they were still some fifty yards from the exit, Ben clearly discerned three shadowy figures walking into the light of the tunnel's opening. He shut off his flashlight. It was obvious the outlined bodies belonged to two men and a woman. One of the men was leaning severely to the left, favoring his right leg. The other stood alone to the side. The woman wore a tattered dress, with stringy hair covering half of her skull. The terrifying trio stopped, and then, as if choreographed, they raised their decaying faces and began shuffling into the darkness toward Ben and Crystal. Collectively, they sensed the presence and scent of humans.

"Not again," Ben mumbled.

Crystal froze, holding on tightly to her boyfriend.

"Ben, what do we do?"

"Shhh! Don't make a sound!"

Ben looked behind him, momentarily entertaining the idea of retreating back into the bowels of the tunnel. It was a stupid thought, and he knew it. There was no way out.

"Prepared and protected," he thought. *Right, Dad. And once again, I'm neither!*

The couple stood like two dark statues, as rigid as the granite rock surrounding them. Ben could feel the moisture of Crystal's sweating hand.

"What are we gonna do?" she whispered.

"I'm working on it."

Ben calculated how long it would take the three ghouls to trudge their way to where he and Crystal were. He was doing the math on how long he had to live.

The female zombie let out a devilish screech, followed by a low growl from the others. They were coming faster now.

What are my options here? Ben wondered. *I have zero protection. No means of escape and no retreat. All I have is a set of car keys, a flashlight, and some ChapStick. Not to mention a girl who is about to go ape crazy in two minutes.*

He squeezed Crystal's hand. They looked at each other, their faces now barely visible in the fading daylight.

"Ben, we're gonna die, aren't we? I don't want to die, baby. I'm not ready," she said, her voice quivering.

"We're not going to die," Ben answered calmly, while at the same time thinking, *We're gonna die. And there's absolutely nothing I can do about it. Then we're gonna come back as one of them. And there's nothing I can do about* that *either!*

The three flesh-eaters were now twenty yards away and still coming. An unbearable stench, carried along by the tunnel breeze, forced its way up the couple's nostrils. But for the zombies, Ben and Crystal emanated an appetizing aroma. They were so close now that Ben could distinguish their features. These beasts were advanced in years, and their clothes were what you'd expect grandparents to wear. Even so, age was no issue, as all reanimated corpses possess superhuman strength.

"Crystal, when I count to three, I want you to run as fast as you can to your left, then toward the entrance."

"But what are you gonna—?"

"Just *do* it!" he snapped, squeezing her hand so hard it hurt. There was a pause; then Ben began counting,

"One . . . two . . . three! GO!"

Ben gave his girlfriend a shove. She took off along the wall, screaming as she ran. Barely slipping past the female zombie, she began a frantic race toward the dimming light outside. The three ghastly creatures instinctively turned in the direction of

Crystal's escape, and the female zombie went after her. The others renewed their pursuit of the fresh brains inside Ben's head. But Ben Forman had no intention of being eaten this day, all alone inside Braxton's Tunnel. The twenty-four-year-old summoned his courage, then uncharacteristically roared at the flesh-monsters, matching their growls with one of his own. Sprinting directly toward the one on his right, he collided with such force that the zombie's arm severed at the shoulder, splashing into a stagnant puddle. Ben swung his flashlight, landing a crushing blow to the temple. The impact shattered both the light's lens and the zombie's skull. The creature fell against the granite wall, his decomposing head caving in like an eggshell. This enraged the remaining male. Though advanced in age, he had a powerful presence about him. An almost demonic aura. He snarled and lunged forward, but Ben dodged him. This split-second miss was the window of opportunity Ben was hoping for. He hurled the flesh-stained flashlight at the powerful old monster and bolted toward the light as fast as his Chuck Taylors would carry him.

The walking cadaver moaned angrily, pivoting in his tracks. Ben raced past the remaining female and made it to the entrance. Crystal threw her arms around him and began crying.

"We don't have time for this," Ben said, trying to catch his breath. "We have to get out of here. NOW!"

The couple raced through the woods like frightened deer. Ben fumbled with his keys before finally opening the car door. Hyperventilating and with hands trembling in sweaty fear, he nervously shoved the key into the ignition and cranked the engine. Jerking the car into gear, he slammed the accelerator, spewing a spray of dirt, gravel, and leaves from beneath his tires.

Crystal locked her door as Ben cast a quick glance up into his rearview mirror. Emerging from the surrounding woods

were dozens upon dozens of the living dead. They had awakened a whole colony of zombies, and their foul presence now
filled the forest.

Exiting the gravel lot, Ben's tires gripped pavement, leaving
smoke and a long, black streak on the lonely mountain road.

"Ben?"

"Yeah, what is it?"

"Babe, you're . . . bleeding."

Chapter 11

DYING TO LIVE

I have been crucified with Christ and I no longer live, but Christ lives in me. The life I live in the body, I live by faith in the Son of God, who loved me and gave himself for me.

—**The Apostle Paul**[1]

Jesus and the Old Sweater

In my almost three decades of ministry, I've come to a conclusion. People don't "bail on Jesus" because they tried him and found the experience unfulfilling. On the contrary, after admitting their lives were a dead end, they really did discover a profound peace, an amazing joy, and a confident hope in a relationship with the Christ. They no longer feared death. They gained a new family of friends. They learned all kinds of mind-blowing things about this God—stuff they had distantly heard from preachers, parents, and youth pastors in the past. But now they've embraced these truths for themselves. They found out that neither their boyfriends/girlfriends, husbands/

wives, or jobs/careers was the "magic formula" they had been searching for. Instead, they had found—and been found by—the Author of life itself. They became believers, and started to own their own faith. They were fulfilled. Satisfied for the first time in their lives. They had a Savior.

But then they encountered something they hadn't anticipated. Something that gradually snuck up on them amid the soul celebration they'd been enjoying. It soon built in strength, and before long it swelled into a tsunami of resistance from within. Something inside each of them didn't like this change of heart, this new perspective and lifestyle transformation. The old tenant doesn't like the heart's new occupant. This new inhabitant has been cleaning house, rearranging furniture, throwing away junk that has been horded for years. He's restocked the library, discarding a lifetime of trash that had filled its shelves. He has cleaned out the refrigerator, replacing spoiled food with fresh groceries. He turned over the bed, revealing the filth that has been hidden underneath it. He removed trophies from the mantel, and everything related to self-accomplishment and pride. He fumigated the basement, ridding it of the putrid, foul stench that has permeated that space for so long.

Then this new resident crossed the line, announcing to the old tenant that he is no longer welcome in this home. He will have to give up his seat on the couch where he has spent years commanding the affairs of the household.

And *that's* usually when people decide that being a committed follower of Jesus isn't all it's cracked up to be. They had assumed that since they had found a Savior, life was going to be "all better" now. Jesus was their ticket to heaven. Their new Buddy. Their God-given good-luck charm. But the charm has worn off. Reality has kicked in, and the buzz they got from the initial experience is fading fast. They quickly discover that there are no standing ovations for their decision to pursue a relationship with the Son of God. They enjoyed the encouragement they got from their Christian friends early on, but they soon learned that Christians aren't always around. Worse, not everyone is as excited about their faith as their fellow believers are. Some people shake their heads. Some have laughed or mocked them. Others avoid them.

But the worst experience of all occurs when they are alone. They begin noticing a different attitude in themselves. A change on the inside. The excitement they once felt while around other disciples has been replaced by feelings of weakness. They find it is difficult to follow Jesus at all times. It's hard to do the right thing when they are alone. Sometimes it even seems impossible. Sometimes they don't even want to believe. They begin wondering if all of this is real, or if it was simply a phase they were going through—like changing majors in college, or switching boyfriends, or like the time they aspired to be a professional musician or artist. Something within them doesn't like this Jesus activity, so it has begun a campaign to convince them to turn back. It reminds them of how great things were back in the day. How much easier life was. Ignoring the crises and chaos that marked their lives before Christ, their minds play a highlight reel of past good times and laughter. A digital photo album of happy memories. Clips of friends and fun parties. Of doing what they wanted to. But all that has changed now, and they find themselves longing for the way things used to be. So Jesus gets shoved into a drawer along with that old sweater that doesn't fit anymore.

And the old tenant glares through an outside window, and smiles.

Ground Control

People don't bail on Jesus because he let them down or because they didn't find him interesting or fulfilling. They walk away because the wicked living dead within them finds the whole "Christ thing" detestable. God wants to be in charge now, and that simply won't do.

While on earth, Jesus talked about these kinds of people. He told a story about a farmer who scattered a bag of seeds on the ground. Some seed got eaten up on the path almost as soon as it hit the ground. Other seed landed in rocky places where there wasn't much soil. The sun came up and scorched it because it had no depth. Other seeds fell among thorns, which grew up and choked the plants, killing any potential fruit. And then some seed landed in good soil; it developed roots, grew, and produced an amazing crop.[2]

I've known lots of people who are open to the thought of life with God. Atheists, agnostics, those with alternative life-styles—they've all come to our church, impressed by the love, shocked at how normal and "un-churchy" we are, attracted to the relevancy and powerful simplicity of the message. But their openness to God-stuff rarely lasts very long. The enemy makes sure of that. And they move on. I have been friends with many others who "get all excited" about Jesus, so enthusiastic you could power an aircraft carrier with their energy. They come on strong, buy a new Bible, tell all their friends about God, gather faithfully with other believers at church, join Bible studies, and even show up to serve. But when the truth of God's Word starts messing with their character or meddling with their heart attitudes, they make up an excuse to bail, usually blaming the church or other Christians. Some walk away because other things have choked out the life Christ offers them—competing priorities, the pursuit of money, relationships, addictions, or the sin nature's old desires—these are allowed to reoccupy the seat of honor in their heart.

And then some, and it's usually a small percentage, deeply embrace the truth of God and his right to reign in their lives. And though they still encounter a daily struggle with sin and self, they choose to continue in him. One day at a time.

So is Jesus just a phase? A passing fad of faith? A season of spirituality? Is that all he is to you? Is he merely a chapter or two in your story? Or is he the Author of it? Is he an extended scene in your life's highlight film? And how would you know? How will you answer that question in five years?

Paul was well aware of the struggle you and I face. He understood and experienced the consistent, powerful pull downward. That's why he wanted you to understand and believe the truth about your sin nature having been "crucified" (rendered powerless). That it has no legal right or authority to control you any longer. Acceptance of that core truth is critical. You have to believe it, and believe it every day.

But there is something else Paul wants us to know. Something that literally makes the difference between survival and defeat in the Christian life. If you could have a live chat with the apostle Paul, it might go something like this:

YOU: So, Paul, what's the real secret to keeping my inner zombie in check? How do I keep it from consuming me every day?

PAUL: Well, you have to learn to "let go and walk."

YOU: "Let go and walk"? What's that supposed to mean? Let go of what?

PAUL: You have to stop being in charge of your own life. You have to let go of the controls and the right to rule yourself.

YOU: What does that look like?

PAUL: When I wrote my Christian friends in Ephesus, I put it this way: "Don't be drunk with wine, because that will ruin your life. Instead, be filled with the Holy Spirit."[3]

YOU: What do drinking wine and the Holy Sprit have in common? You're losing me here.

PAUL: Think about it. When someone is drunk, the alcohol influences everything about him. And how is a drunk person affected? His vision is blurred or hindered. His judgment is impaired. His speech is slurred. His personality is altered. Muscle coordination reduced. Under the influence of alcohol, you do things you might not ordinarily do. It influences what comes out of your mouth. You lose certain inhibitions. It affects your relationships. It changes you. So by drinking too much wine, you essentially give the alcohol permission to direct and influence your mind, body, and choices. It greatly influences your behavior and everything about you.

YOU: I've seen drunk people. I know what you're talking about. So you're saying I should allow the Holy Spirit to influence me like alcohol does a drunk person.

PAUL: Yes, in the sense that you release yourself to be under his direction and control.

YOU: And when that happens, I will be different?

PAUL: Absolutely. By surrendering control, you will be under his influence and authority.

YOU: But it's not like some kind of mystical "trance" thing, right?

PAUL: No, not at all. God wants to be in charge of

us and our personalities, but he doesn't take our personalities away. Instead, he works through them. He hard-wired your personality, and still wants you to be you, only with him in charge.

YOU: So how do I become filled with the Holy Spirit? Is there a prayer I have to pray or some formula to recite?

PAUL: Of course not. Remember, you're in a relationship with a personal God. He isn't a math equation. He's a Person. Simply choose to let him take charge of you. Let go. It will change your relationships and attitudes about life.[4]

YOU: Then it's simply a choice I make, right?

PAUL: Yep. But not always an easy one, because your inner zombie will try to resist. But you have to remind yourself that the thing within no longer has any authority in your life. So simply give up your right to be in charge of yourself.

YOU: And how often should I do this?

PAUL: As often as you feel the need to. Whenever you've sinned. Whenever you need strength, help, or direction. Whenever you're facing problems. Many times a day. And in time, it will become as natural as breathing . . . or as natural as walking.

YOU: Yeah, walking was the second thing you mentioned. What does that mean?

PAUL: I admonished my friends in Galatia this way: "Walk by the Spirit, and you will not gratify the desires of the flesh."[5] Think about walking for a minute. When you were born, you didn't know how to walk. Or even crawl. You couldn't even hold your own head up. But over time, you learned to walk, falling a lot in the process. Through practice, you learned how to put one foot in front of the other, keeping your balance, and over time it became second nature to you. Now you get up each day and walk without thinking about it. That's how we learn to walk with God. As we surrender to him throughout each day, we end up following where he leads us. Walking by the power of the Spirit allows us to experience the amazing life Jesus promised us.[6] And as you continue giving him first place each day, you begin intuitively knowing what he wants you to do.[7] It's a relationship, and a process.

YOU: But sometimes I feel like the path I'm walking on is uphill, rocky, and filled with potholes and land mines.

PAUL: You got that right. That's why you have to keep your eyes on where the Lord is walking. Place your foot where he places his.[8] Follow his lead. And stay close to him at all times. Remember, you have enemies who want to trip you up or blow you up. Plus, you have an inner nemesis who doesn't want to be evicted.

YOU: Sounds like warfare to me.

PAUL: Exactly.

• • •

So, never forget that your identity is in Christ. You belong to him—by right and by choice. He is responsible for your salvation and your daily survival. You are responsible to surrender to him and, by his power, to follow his lead. This involves a long-term growth process, so don't become frustrated. It's a battle you and I will fight till we arrive in heaven. I'm still learning every day what it means to surrender to his control and follow my benevolent Master. But if you and I take life one day at a time, we can continue in him with the confidence that he will finish the beautiful masterpiece he began in us.[9]

HOW TO KILL
A ZOMBIE

Ben, are you hurt? Did they touch you, babe?" Crystal asked.

"Huh? Oh, that. I just scraped my hand. It's nothing."

Ben reported what he had seen at the tunnel to the authorities. A ZTF team was dispatched to the area, and by morning, seventy-seven walking dead had been hunted down and destroyed, though it was unclear if they had gotten them all. Ben had dropped Crystal off at a girlfriend's for the night, and once back at his apartment, he texted Dan.

> I'm thinking about buying a gun.
> Suggestions?

Ben waited, but there was no response. He went to bed, but not before moving a dining room table against his apartment door. And wedging a chair under the doorknob in his bedroom. Before drifting off to sleep, he wondered, *God, if you're really there, why don't you stop this curse?*

219

The next morning, he was awakened at six thirty by a text.

```
I'll see you Thursday at Mom's and
            we'll talk.
```

Ben had to think before remembering what he had texted Dan the night before. Guns were Dan's thing, not Ben's. Nevertheless, he was convinced that, sooner or later, if he did not take the necessary precautions, his luck would run out and he'd suffer the same fate as Kyle, his dad, and the man in the alley. No more being unprepared and unprotected.

● ● ●

Thanksgiving morning arrived, and soon Ben and Crystal were passing through the large steel gate and driving up the winding lane to Patricia Forman's house. Dan's truck was in the driveway.

"I can't wait for you to meet my brother."

Crystal smiled.

The motorized stairway was lowering as Ben pulled his car into the driveway. Dan was waiting at the top, dressed in khakis and a black sweater.

"It's about time," Dan blurted out.

Ben shook his head as he and Crystal climbed the stairs. The two brothers bear-hugged, with Dan lifting Ben off the deck floor.

"Dan," he said, still being squeezed, "this is my girlfriend, Crystal."

Dan dropped his brother.

"Crystal, it's so nice to finally meet you." He gave her a hug.

"You too. Ben talks about you all the time. It's good to put a name with a face ... or a face with a name ... however that goes."

"Well, he told me you were beautiful. And I have to say, he was dead-on. You're gorgeous."

"Well, thank you, Dan. You're very kind," Crystal said, blushing.

Dan put his arm around his brother's shoulder. "Let's go inside. It's freezing out here."

Once inside, Dan hit the switch, raising the stairs. Patricia Forman appeared from the kitchen, drying her hands on a dish towel.

"Happy Thanksgiving, son," she said, giving Ben a hug and a kiss on the cheek. She followed up with one for Crystal as well.

"I'm so glad you're here, honey."

"Thank you for inviting me, Mrs. Forman."

"Y'all make yourself comfortable. I've still got pies in the oven to see to."

The three gathered around a small living room table. A fire was crackling in the fireplace, compliments of Dan. The TV above the mantel aired a football game. On the table was a wooden tray filled with nuts. Dan picked up a pecan and began cracking it.

"So, Crystal, tell me about yourself. What do you do?"

"Well, for about nine months I've worked downtown at a coffee shop. But it's just a job."

"The stuff they make at ZTF headquarters is just horrible. I don't know how they get away with calling it coffee."

Crystal laughed. "Well, you know, coffee isn't that hard to make. But we do roast our own beans, so I'm kinda partial to it."

"I should take some of your coffee back with me. So, are you from around here?"

"Just east of the city, actually. A little town called Leesville. When my dad died, we moved—"

Their conversation was cut short as a man entered the

room. He looked about sixty—a short, balding man wearing a white turtleneck under a red cable-knit sweater.

"Hello there," the man said in a cheerful voice. "I'm Phil. Phil Carson."

The three stood to meet him.

"I'm Dan," said the older brother, giving the man a firm handshake.

Phil smiled pleasantly and then turned to the younger Forman son. "And you must be Ben."

"Yessir. Nice to meet you. And this is my girlfriend, Crystal."

"It's a pleasure to meet all of you. Pat can't stop talking about her boys. I met your mom here a few months back. I just live six houses down the hill."

Appearing with a hot pie in her hands, Patricia Forman broke into their conversation.

"I'm sorry, Ben. I told Dan but forgot to mention to you that Phil was already here. He's been lying down in the guest room. He's been feeling a little under the weather lately."

Patricia paused, then announced, "Well, I think we're ready to eat. I've asked Phil to say a prayer, and then Dan will do the carving."

The fivesome gathered around the dinner table, adjacent to the living room. Phil's prayer was predictable. Nevertheless, Patricia complimented him on it. Then, seated at the head of the table, Dan picked up a carving knife and large fork. "Okay, let's butcher this bird."

The dinner conversation was lively and upbeat, with the boys politely grilling Phil Carson with questions. They discovered that he was a semiretired entrepreneur who'd patented several inventions, including a wind-up revolving spaghetti fork. The concept never took off, and Carson admitted that he still had boxes of them collecting dust in his attic. He had two grown daughters, he said, who live in Oklahoma, and his wife passed away from cancer five years ago. Phil seemed like a nice enough guy, laughed a lot, and was somewhat of a handyman. While passing the gravy, Patricia spotted her boys giving each other a silent look of approval. Phil had passed the test.

After dinner, Crystal helped Mrs. Forman clear the table, while Phil excused himself, disappearing once again into the guest bedroom for another nap. Dan grabbed his backpack.

"Ben, join me on the deck for a minute."

Once outside, Ben remarked, "Phil seems like a nice guy."

"You mean Rip Van Winkle? Yeah, I think he's harmless. I'm just glad Mom has a friend. She deserves the company."

"Yeah," Ben agreed.

"Okay, so I've been thinking about your question, Ben."

"Huh?"

"You know. About getting a gun."

"Oh, *that*. Sure. So, what do you think?"

Dan unzipped his pack. "I want to show you something." He drew out a shiny, just-polished weapon.

"What's this?" Ben asked his brother.

"Well, what does it look like?" Dan shot back. "It's a pistol." He handed the gun, nearly identical to the one he'd given his dad, to Ben, but not before clearing the chamber.

"*Niiiice*," Ben said, holding it in his hands as if weighing it. "How much are you selling it for?"

"It's not for sale." Dan smiled. "It's yours. Merry *early* Christmas, little brother. Don't say I never gave you anything."

"First off, stop calling me 'little brother' or I'm gonna hit you. And second, there's no way I can take this . . . Are you serious?"

"You have to take it. It's a gift. Just promise you'll keep it clean. That one was given to me. It's special. But hey, so are you. So take care of yourself with it."

"Gosh, Dan. I really don't know what to say."

"No need for a speech. There are a few boxes of .45s in there too."

• • •

While this moment of brotherly bonding was going on, some-thing else was happening a quarter mile away. Thanksgiving brought more than normal traffic to Farmington Heights. After opening the large steel gate, the security officer saw a car enter, then suddenly stop. He immediately left his guard-house to check on the vehicle. He tapped on the driver's-side window, and it lowered, revealing an elderly woman, crying and badly bleeding.

"Ma'am, you're gonna have to move this . . . Hey, are you all right?" The guard leaned forward to offer assistance while reaching for his shoulder radio to call for backup. But before he could relay his message, he was violently pulled through the window by a large man in the passenger seat, who then proceeded to devour him alive. Within minutes, the half-eaten security guard reanimated and finished off the old woman as she screamed in vain for help. From behind the immobile car, more zombies shuffled along the road leading to Farmington Heights. Out of the woods they came, as if beckoned for a Thanksgiving feast of their own.

A guard on the east tower wall noticed the open gate but from his vantage point could not see the events taking place behind it. He radioed the gate guardhouse, but received no reply. He then contacted the security bunker, and a guard was sent up to check it out. This man disappeared behind the steel gate—and was instantly attacked and eaten. The tower guard then did the only thing he knew to do.

He hit the alarm.

The gated community's breached-security alarm blared like a World War II air-raid siren. It was reserved for one reason only. Zombies.

Immediately, the compound went into lockdown mode. An override switch kicked in, and the large steel gate automatically began closing, but was prevented from doing so by the stalled car. Three tower guards abandoned their posts to move it, but were quickly repelled by a throng of ghouls, forcing their retreat back up into the safety of their towers. More creatures poured through the opening, like water through a broken dam.

•••

Dan and Ben, still on the deck, heard the siren and rushed inside, locking the door. Meanwhile, Farmington's bunker command center had already sent messages to all residents' computers and phones, warning them of the breach.

Lock down. Lock down. Lock down. This is not a test!

Pat accessed the security cams via the website. They revealed clumps of wandering zombies clambering around the base of the first few towers. "It's *them*," she said, her voice barely above a whisper. The siren's wail climbed up the sloping valley, echoing off the mountain.

Phil Carson bolted out of the guest bedroom, hysterical and drenched in sweat. "Wha-what's happening? What's going on? Where's Pat?"

"I'm here, Phil," she assured him. "Dear, you don't look well. Are you feeling all right?"

"This isn't supposed to happen!" he shouted. And with those words, Carson fell facedown onto the carpeted floor. Patricia rushed to his side, and Dan took his vital signs.

"He's just passed out, but he's burning up with fever. Let's get him to the couch. Ben, give me a hand."

Patricia motioned to Crystal. "Honey, run and get me a wet washrag from the hall bathroom."

After moving Phil to the couch, Ben went to the window. "I don't see anything. Shouldn't there be security guards running around or something?"

"I don't know, baby. But they told us if the big siren goes off, we're supposed to get to the first floor immediately."

"Soon," Dan responded. "But first, I need to get to my truck."

"Not on your life, Dan Forman!" his mother declared. "You're not going outside until that siren stops and we're sure it's safe!"

Ben returned to check the security cams. "There's no one anywhere around the house, Mom."

"Mom, I know what I'm doing here," Dan said. "I'll be back in less than sixty seconds. Trust me, all right? Ben, I need you on the stairs."

The brothers hurried onto the deck, but not before Dan popped a magazine into the pistol he'd just given Ben. "Mind if I borrow this for a minute?" he asked.

Ben was surprised at how calm he felt, maybe because Dan was there. He hit the switch, and the motorized stairs soon touched down. Dan descended and sprinted to his truck. Pulling back the seat, he grabbed another backpack and a pump shotgun. He also stuffed a two-way radio into his pants. Slamming the truck door, Dan turned to head back toward the house, when he was suddenly confronted by a very tall zombie. The lurching ghoul was about 6 feet, 10 inches tall wearing sweats and untied basketball shoes. Dan didn't miss a beat, slamming the giant across the jaw with the butt of his shotgun.

"No more hoops for you, pal," he declared as the jaw flew across the yard and the creature began an awkward roll down the driveway, smashing his head on the mailbox post.

Dan leapt up the stairs, shouting, "Bring it up, Ben!"

With the stairs securely locked in place, the boys retreated back inside.

"Just to be on the safe side, shouldn't we barricade the door?" Ben suggested.

"Good call," Dan said.

Uncharacteristically calm, Crystal helped move a china cabinet against the house's only exit. Phil Carson moaned from the couch, a wet washrag draped across his sweaty forehead. Dan stared at him from across the room, stroking his chin.

"Okay, this is what we're going to do. Mom, where's Dad's pistol? And my old .22 rifle?"

"They're both in the guest bedroom closet, honey."

"Good. Ben, go get them, and any ammo you can find."

"Won't somebody get me something for this head-ache?!" Phil shouted from the couch. Patricia went to the kitchen, retrieving a pain reliever. Ben returned with the handgun and rifle.

"I got two boxes of .45s and a bag of .22s."

"All right. For now, we're going to conserve our ammo. Let's see how bad things get first. I'm sure there's been an alert at headquarters, and teams are on their way. So we just need to hang tight for now."

"But don't they notify you when there's an alert?" Ben asked.

"Since I'm on leave, the guys on post are the only ones who know about it right now."

Privately, though, Dan wondered why he hadn't heard any chatter on his radio.

"This thing will probably be over before morning. We just have to be patient and prepared for a lot of gunfire when my ZTF boys get here."

Phil Carson lingered on the couch, his sock feet propped up and his portly waistline rising and falling with each breath. Though quieter now, his face told the story of a man in a lot of pain. Dan was keeping an eye on him.

Suddenly the ear-piercing siren stopped, and the only sound was crowd noise from the football game on TV. Dan walked over and turned it off.

"What does *that* mean?" Crystal inquired. "Is it over?"

Dan quickly answered, "This thing is far from over. Since I've yet to hear gunfire, I'm assuming the security here has failed. We can't depend on those rent-a-guards out there to protect us. It's in *our* hands now."

No sooner had he said those words than the power went out.

"Time to head downstairs!" Dan announced.

What the dinner party could not have known was that a grave error had occurred inside the underground command center. Monitoring the events happening above them, a technician panicked. Seeking to escape and go to his family, he stupidly released the air lock on the single bunker exit to make a run for his car. Hidden from his sight were some forty zombies near the bunker door. He never had a chance. The beasts poured down the stairs. The other technicians, untrained in firearms, foolishly began firing the emergency automatic weapons stored there. Haphazardly spraying bullets across the control room, they disabled the alarm and electrical systems. Within minutes the men were out of ammunition. With the power grid crippled, they suffered a most *horrible* death—eaten alive in the dark by a swarm of ravenous flesh-eaters.

Their screams unheard.

• • •

Patricia, preparing to go downstairs, helped Phil into a sitting position.

"No, Mom," Dan declared. "Not him."

"What? Daniel, what are you talking about? We have to get downstairs. You said so."

"I'm sorry, Mom. Phil could be showing early signs of stage 2, and we can't take that chance."

"But Dan," his mother pleaded, "we can't just leave him up here all alone. He's sick."

"I just have a touch of the flu, that's all," Carson protested, attempting a cough.

"That may be, Mr. Carson. And if so, you'll be okay up here. There's no access to this level. But if not, you put all our lives in danger. Sorry, but that's not a risk I'm willing to take. Besides, by morning we'll know more either way."

"Morning? Dan!" his mother begged. "You can't do this! I forbid it!"

"Mom!" Ben interjected. "We need to trust Dan here. Besides, his plan protects all of us."

"We're wasting time. Let's go," Dan ordered.

Ben and Crystal headed to the hallway door leading downstairs. Patricia gave Phil a hug.

"Just go," he reassured her. "I'll be fine up here."

Patricia reluctantly left the couch and walked toward the downstairs door, but not before giving her son a disapproving glare.

Dan looked over at Phil once more.

"Just rest for now. There's juice in the kitchen. And . . . well, we'll see you in the morning."

Once downstairs, the men shut the reinforced door, bolting the three huge bars securely in place.

"Let's get the generator started, Ben. We'll need the air-filtration system running as a precaution. Besides, these battery lights won't last long."

Crystal looked at Ben, who assured her that everything was going to be okay.

Dan positioned Ben and himself at the front wall, while Patricia monitored the back. The three windows were, in reality, cross-shaped slits in the cinder-block wall, more reminiscent of what would appear on a medieval castle than on a modern home design.

Dan handed his mom the pistol he'd previously given his dad. "You know what to do with this, Mom. Remember, they can't get down here, but ammo is limited, so make your shots count. Head shots only.

"And I believe this one's yours, Ben," he said, giving the other .45 back to his brother. Ben chambered a round into his new pistol while Dan readied the rifle and shotgun.

"I wonder if this is happening anywhere else," Crystal said.

Silence ruled the next thirty minutes. Patricia worried about Phil's condition upstairs, while Dan wondered when he would hear the roar of helicopter blades. He'd been unable to reach anyone on his two-way, and now none of their phones were getting signals. Ben stood at his window post, carefully scanning the valley below.

"Where the heck are they?" he said.

Then, around four that afternoon, Patricia heard something. "What was that?" she asked.

"Mom. Quiet!" Ben whispered.

"It's okay, Ben. They'll smell us long before they hear us. What'd you hear, Mom?"

"Something upstairs. We have to go check on Phil!"

"You know we can't do that. Phil's fine, I'm sure he's just—"

BOOM! . . . BOOM! . . . BOOM!

The muted thuds came from the door of their first-floor bunker. Patricia dashed toward the door. "Phil? PHIL? Is that you?" she cried.

A muffled voice replied, "Yes, it's me. You have to let me down there, now!"

"We're not gonna do that, Phil!" Ben shouted.

"But you *have* to. Before it's too late!" Carson begged.

"In the morning, Phil," Dan said. "When we're certain you're not . . . when we're sure everything's safe."

"You fools!" Phil shouted. "By then we'll all be dead! Can't you see?"

"See *what*?" Dan yelled.

"The kitchen window! The kitchen window!" Carson cried. "They're *coming*!"

Since there was no corresponding window downstairs, the first-floor occupants had no field of vision eastward. Dan and Ben scanned their openings, still seeing nothing.

Dan headed toward the door. "Phil, I need you to go back upstairs and take another look. Then come back and tell us how many you see."

"No need," Ben said from his window post. "I can tell you. There are hundreds! Maybe more!"

Dan raced to the window again. Scores of zombies were staggering up the hill like a tottering army marching in formation. Closer and closer they came.

"Don't shoot," Dan commanded. "Not yet."

"Open this door, and let me down there!" Phil pleaded. "I'm weak, and I have no way of protecting myself."

Patricia began to sob quietly, her forehead pressed against the door.

Ben tightened his grip on the pistol Dan had given him. He noticed his hands weren't sweating. As the throng inched within firing range, Ben's eyes were drawn toward one zombie in particular. He was old, wearing shabby clothing, like a vagrant. As he drew closer, Ben recognized him as the zombie from the tunnel. His right foot was bare and horribly mutilated; but on his left foot was a black Converse shoe, its white tip stained in crimson.

"No way," Ben whispered. "That's *my* shoe!"

"Mom, I really need you on that north wall!" Dan shouted. But Patricia remained at the bolted door, her thoughts focused on her sick friend.

"Ben?" Crystal asked her boyfriend. "What do I do in all this?"

"Just sit tight for now—"

"And pray," Patricia interrupted. "Pray to God."

"Some prayer wouldn't hurt," Dan agreed.

That comment got Patricia's attention. Turning her tear-filled eyes toward her oldest son, she took the pistol and without a word resumed her post at the north window.

The sounds on the other side of the basement door suddenly ceased. This normally signified the brief pause that occurs between stage 2 and the full rage of stage 3. Only time would tell. Meanwhile, the rotting horde lunged forward, their stench arriving yards ahead of them.

With guns loaded and cocked, Dan spoke. "Well, happy Thanksgiving."

"Yeah," Ben replied. "Some Thanksgiving."

"So, you ready for this, little brother?"

Ben looked intently at the soldier, nodding confidently.

"All right, flesh addicts," Dan said. "Come get some."

Ben breathed calmly, aimed at the one-shoed zombie, and pulled the trigger. The bullet found its target, smashing into the creature's skull, catapulting him backward. Firing round after round, he and Dan kept reloading, and the zombies kept coming. Before long, the brothers had eliminated several waves of the living dead, and it seemed like they had destroyed them all. Still, Dan couldn't shake the haunting feeling that this was only the beginning of something much bigger.

● ● ●

And now, six months later, I, Dan Forman, sit here on my bunk at ZTF headquarters, cleaning my weapon and preparing for yet another mission. It's become a full-scale outbreak now. Just like so many had warned about. But no one could have predicted how many lives would be lost. And how close to home this war would come. The alarm on my watch says it's time to load up.

They're everywhere now. God help us.

Chapter 12

THE COMING ZOMBIE APOCALYPSE

I am coming soon! My reward is with me.
—Jesus[1]

Careful What You Wish For

The future is as mysterious as it is intriguing. Speculations of what life on earth will be like in the coming days are in no short supply, providing us with just as many future fantasies as nightmares. And some are downright creepy. No doubt you have a favorite book or movie related to this genre. But as entertaining as that movie or novel may be, it's still just a made-up story. Pure fantasy. Though no one has definitively figured out all the details about what is popularly known as the "end times," here's what we do know. The Bible makes it clear that prior to the return of Jesus Christ to this planet, things are going to get really bad down here.

I mean, *really* bad.

Paul warned his young pastor friend, "But mark this: There will be terrible times in the last days. People will be lovers of themselves, lovers of money, boastful, proud, abusive, disobedient to their parents, ungrateful, unholy, without love, unforgiving, slanderous, without self-control, brutal, not lovers of the good, treacherous, rash, conceited, lovers of pleasure rather than lovers of God—having a form of godliness but denying its power. Have nothing to do with them."[2]

Looking at this description, does it seem to you that humanity's collective inner zombie is being released on one another, resulting in a world gone mad? According to the Bible, unchecked self-worship will ultimately one day produce global moral insanity. Anarchy at home. Hateful, malicious, out-of-control living by ego-driven, insatiable pursuers of pleasure. Sounds like a plot for the next futuristic feature film. Things are not getting better here on planet Earth. They're getting worse. But the informed Christ-follower should already know this. We already discovered that our sin nature continually decays in its moral decadence.[3]

But what could possibly push mankind over the edge like this? Is it some cataclysmic event or strange worldwide occurrence? It stands to reason that as the standard of morality continues to break down worldwide, more and more people will take advantage of the opportunity. Building like floodwaters of sin against a dam of decency and character, the corruption will advance, and soon there will come a time when the dam can keep it back no longer.

When Paul wrote to his friends at Thessalonica, he gave them hope that they would one day see their fellow believers who had died. This hope, he said, is found in the return of Jesus. At that time he'll snatch up his bride before pouring out judgment on a Christ-rejecting planet. This event is popularly known as the "Rapture,"[4] and Paul wrote about it in 1 Thessalonians 4:16–17: "For the Lord himself will come down from heaven, with a loud command, with the voice of the archangel and with the trumpet call of God, and the dead in Christ will rise first. After that, we who are still alive and are left will be caught up together with them in the clouds to meet the Lord in the air. And so we will be with the Lord forever." This event is critical to what takes place in the end times for one huge reason—every Christian (along with the Holy Spirit living inside them) will now be absent from this world. And with the Holy Spirit gone, there is no more righteous influence through God's children in society or culture. Imagine if all Christians were removed from government, or if there were no believers in schools or universities. No Christian doctors, lawyers, business owners, scientists, writers, actors, or musicians. All of them gone. Vanished. Extinct. No one promoting a Judeo-Christian ethic or morality. No one championing the causes of the underprivileged. Truly a Christ-less world.

Humanity has no idea how much it owes Christ's followers. How sad that many see us only as "right-wing, fundamentalist, narrow-minded bigots" (though this is true of many Christians). But it's also sad that they fail to see all the good Christians have done for the world—feeding the hungry, caring for the orphan, assisting the impoverished, and creating a climate of civility and morality. But at this Rapture, all that will be gone. I've often explained my definition of college as "all your wild friends in one place for four years . . . without their parents." Now imagine that same university campus without the commonsense rules of the administration. No dorm rules. No academic ethic standards. No restrictions regarding males and females. No Christian ministries. Not one person on campus who fears God or trusts in the Messiah.

In this new world without Jesus followers, there will be little to hold back the selfish pursuits and pleasures of a godless world. And God's wrath will be released. But this will be no sudden divine temper tantrum. The Lord is patient, and extremely tolerant and kind. Further, he has given mankind more than two thousand years to hear the truth about his Son. But his patience is coming to an abrupt end. It will run out and then be no more. The dam will burst, unleashing heaven's fury on a rebellious planet. And a big part of this judgment involves God releasing humanity to itself, giving it what it has always wanted—a world without him.

Think about that for a minute.

People should be careful what they wish for.

Hell on Earth

You would think the sudden disappearance of millions of people all over the world would drive humanity to its knees, begging God for forgiveness. But just the opposite will happen, the Bible tells us. Not only will men curse God for the judgments that follow,[5] but God will further judge them by sending them a "powerful delusion,"[6] which will cause them to believe the lies fed to them. Considering the consequences of this many people vanishing, they'll have a whole new reason to hate us. The disappearance of every single Christian at the Rapture will surely produce initial worldwide panic. Catastrophes, countless plane and car crashes, family members snatched away, teachers gone, doctors disappeared, employees evaporated out of sight. Every stratum of society will suffer loss. Top to bottom. Every neighborhood affected. Mortgages, car payments, credit cards, and student loans have no way to be paid. This will trigger a massive financial crisis, sending a shockwave of panic through governments across the globe. Will there be rioting in the streets? Governments overthrown? Revolutions? Wars?

We call it the "Rapture." Perhaps those left behind will refer to it as "the Great Vanishing."

This phenomenon might be explained to the rest of

humanity as a colossal alien abduction or perhaps even a judgment-gift from God above. "The world," they may claim, "is a better place without all those Christ-fanatics." And it's conceivable that religious groups will rejoice, citing this event as proof that Christianity wasn't good for the world. And it will all somehow make sense.

In this post-rapture scenario, every city becomes "Sin City." Every human becomes the walking dead, completely devoid of God's presence once made known around them. They are completely left to themselves. You think the world is messed up now? Just wait. And don't think for a moment that it can't happen.[7]

At this time, the Bible claims, a certain leader will emerge out of the sea of humanity. This person is called by many names, among them the "man of lawlessness,"[8] the "son of destruction,"[9] the "beast,"[10] and the "prince who is to come."[11] However, the name you probably are familiar with is the "Antichrist."[12] But who is this guy, and what will he be like? According to Scripture, he will emerge as a political leader of a new "one world order." He will have no desire for religion or for women.[13] This will mark an all-time low for humanity. Second Thessalonians tells us this man will exalt himself above everyone, elevating himself to God status, even claiming to be God. He is one of only two people in history to be filled and fully controlled by Satan himself.[14] He is the "anti-Jesus," the ultimate false messiah, the counterfeit Christ. The most evil human being ever.

And the world will swoon over him like a twelve-year-old girl at a Justin Bieber concert.

He will unite the nations and bring temporary economic stability. Meanwhile, the living dead will fill the earth, peddling a new brand of human nobility. But their attempts at anything remotely good will merely be echoes of a previous age. The era when the sin virus was prevented from reaching rage status will officially be over. The Holy Spirit, the Church, conscience, and Christian values in law and government—all gone.

It will be a free-for-all.

But to understand the coming zombie attack, we have to understand another true story.

This kind of thing happened once before in history, and Jesus drew a bone-chilling parallel between Noah's day and the generation immediately leading up to the last days. He said that people will be going about their normal lives, doing the things they always do—eating and drinking, getting married, living for themselves, ignoring God and eternity, just as they'd done in Noah's day. But then Noah entered the ark and the rain began to fall. People were caught completely off guard, their sinful natures having deceived themselves into thinking that Noah was an idiot and the coming flood was a fairy tale.[15] "That is how it will be at the coming of the Son of Man," Jesus warned.[16]

During this final seven-year period on Planet Zombie, there will be fighting, skirmishes, and even wars.[17] But instead of the Hollywood version of ordinary citizens holding off hordes of lumbering zombies, Earth's final battle will be exponentially more horrifying. In the ultimate expression of humanity's hatred of God, all the armies of planet Earth will ally themselves together for a joint war against their common enemy—Jesus the Christ.[18] They'll gather together in what Napoleon called "the world's greatest natural battlefield." Like a gargantuan football field, the Valley of Megiddo (Armageddon) is 280 square miles of prime combat real estate. Millions of soldiers from many nations will rendezvous to wage war against the nail-scarred Savior. But this time, Jesus won't make a humble entrance into the world on a "silent night." There will be no cave births, mangers, or sentimental Christmas songs.

This time he will burst through the clouds, riding triumphantly on a white horse, his redeemed following behind him, also mounted on white horses.[19] His cause is just and his war righteous and holy.[20] This Jesus won't be shedding a compassionate tear, but rather will have eyes that are "flames of fire."[21] Instead of a crown of thorns on his head, there will be many glorious crowns that he has earned. Written on him will be a name that no one knows except himself. A secret tattoo of sorts. He will wear a blood-spattered robe, perhaps a visible reminder of the cross. He will be called "the Word of God,"[22] and from his mouth will come a sharp war-sword. And with it he will slay the nations, filling the great valley with their blood.[23] But there is one more name Jesus will bear at this battle, this one written twice—once on his robe and once on his thigh:

KING OF KINGS AND LORD OF LORDS[24]

This name will be a worldwide declaration of his sovereignty and dominance as God. And miraculously, every person alive will see him return,[25] perhaps through a global simulcast of the event. In an apocalyptic screenplay directed by God himself, hell will come to earth in 3-D. An NC-17 production. Hard to ingest, huh? "But where is the love?" you might ask. "Doesn't love win?"

God does love unconditionally and eternally, and is described as love itself.[26] But we have to embrace the truth that our God is also just and wrathful.[27] And we were once the objects of that wrath, destined for condemnation.[28] It is only because of his rich mercy and mega love that we are made alive in him and spared from the self-curse and hell.[29]

And this epic final battle becomes the crescendo of humanity.

Actually, Armageddon will be more an execution than a battle, as Jesus will slay millions of the walking dead with the word of his mouth. There *will* be blood.

This is your Jesus. Your conquering Hero. Your zombie-killer.

But until that great and terrible day, there is another epic battle raging. It's the one you face at home. At school. In the university dorm. At the office. In the trenches where spirituality meets your reality in a head-on collision. In the warfare of the heart, the conflict rages day by day. It never ceases, and some days are more intense than others.

But remember, you are not a victim in this war. On the contrary, you are destined to win. Defeat may be a part of your experience and history, but it does not mark you or define you. Your true identity is found in Jesus and embracing the person he is making you. You are a warrior, and your Commander is looking you in the eyes right now and calling, *"Follow me."*

"As long as it is day," Jesus said, "we must do the work of him who sent me. Night is coming, when no one can work" (John 9:4).

The coming zombie apocalypse is not a cool, end-times, trendy sci-fi horror movie. It's prophetic reality and a call to get ready. Are you prepared to exit this planet? Are you ready for heaven?

Time is running out, friend, and we who know him must make the most of it for his sake. Contrary to what society or popular culture may say, we are not "basically good." Far from it. Instead, we are corrupt. Broken. Diseased. Dead. *Living dead.* And the scourge of our character cancer haunts us every day.

Our only hope is faith in a Galilean Jew. The Healer. The Giver of hope. The One who claimed to be the Way, Truth, and Life. God's Son. Savior. And he rose from the grave to prove it. Our faith is in he who still performs miracles. And that miracle is in you. That miracle *is* you.

Because God is the Master Storyteller—the ultimate Suspense Novelist—he'll write some irony into your story. Perhaps the twist in this awesome tale is that you don't end up being eaten by your inner zombie after all. Maybe your future lies in being that person who survives when others around you don't make it. Despite the odds, maybe you'll learn the art of combat—winning some days and losing others. I pray you learn the skill of letting go, of releasing your life to him. And in your letting go, you will feel the sun on your face as you walk with him.

Get up and walk while you have the light, before darkness, and the living dead, overtake you.[30]

ACKNOWLEDGMENTS

Taking a book from concept to completion requires a dedicated and competent team of individuals, all working toward a common goal. This book project is no exception. I owe a debt of gratitude to my agent, Bill Jensen, for not disowning me when I conceived and presented a book about zombies to him. Bill's expertise in his profession and belief in me are nothing short of epic. To my editor, Bryan Norman, who enthusiastically saw the enormous potential for life impact *Zombie Killers* could have. His leadership in this project has been stellar. Thanks to the editorial team at Thomas Nelson, who helped refine the final manuscript. A special thanks to the art and design department for their heroic work and awesome talent. And finally, to my son, Stuart, whose editorial input and keen literary insight were invaluable to me in writing this book.

NOTES

Episode One

1. From *The Book*, Origins 3:6. This ancient collection of folklore, spirituality, and teachings is believed by those who subscribe to the Old Way to have been written by God to explain life to them.

Chapter 1

1. Romans 2:14–15.
2. Genesis 1:26–27.
3. Genesis 2:8.
4. Genesis 3:1–7.
5. Genesis 1:26.
6. Isaiah 14; Ezekiel 28.
7. No one knows what type of fruit it was.
8. God killed some animals and clothed the couple with the skins to demonstrate the truth that sin cannot go unpunished (Genesis 3:21).
9. Genesis 6:5–6.
10. Jesus Christ's birth is the only exception to this.

Chapter 2

1. Romans 8:6–8.
2. Isaiah 53:6.
3. Romans 3:10–12.
4. Romans 7:18 NASB.

Chapter 3

1. Romans 3:23.
2. Genesis 8:21; Psalm 51:5; Ephesians 2:2–3.
3. Ephesians 4:22.
4. Romans 7:17–20, 24 MSG.
5. 2 Corinthians 11:24–28.
6. Romans 8:16; Galatians 5:17.

Chapter 4

1. Galatians 5:19–21.
2. 1 Corinthians 5:1–5.
3. Romans 1:24; 2 Corinthians 12:21; Ephesians 5:3; Colossians 3:5.
4. Romans 13:13.
5. 1 Peter 5:8.
6. Ephesians 6:10–12.
7. Romans 8:5; Philippians 4:8.
8. 2 Corinthians 11:2.
9. 1 Corinthians 13:4 NLT, emphasis added.
10. James 3:14, 16.
11. Romans 16:17; 1 Corinthians 3:3.
12. Romans 16:17–18.
13. Romans 1:24–32; 1 Corinthians 6:9–10.

Episode Five

1. The Charter of New Gloucester (1622), preface.

Chapter 5

1. Even though Genesis 25:23 says that Jacob would have gotten the blessing anyway, he shortcut God's plan and made it happen on his own with illegitimate methods.
2. Jeremiah 17:9, emphasis added.
3. Jeremiah 9:4.
4. Hebrews 11:25.
5. Ecclesiastes 2:10–11.
6. Proverbs 4:23.
7. Proverbs 28:26.

Chapter 6

1. John 8:36.
2. Luke 7:41–50.
3. Romans 6:1–2.
4. Hebrews 4:12.

Episode Seven

1. "Death to the dead."

Chapter 7

1. 1 Corinthians 15:33.
2. 1 Corinthians 6:9–11.
3. Romans 8:29.
4. 1 Corinthians 10:12.
5. Mark 14:27.
6. Mark 14:29.
7. Mark 14:30.
8. Mark 14:31.
9. Galatians 2:11–17.
10. Exodus 20:5; see also 2 Corinthians 11:2.
11. Psalm 78:31.

12. 1 John 4:10–11.
13. Zephaniah 3:17.
14. Exodus 34:5–7.
15. Mark 14:34; John 11:35.
16. Genesis 6:5–6; Ephesians 4:30.
17. Ephesians 5:15–32.
18. Proverbs 13:20.

Chapter 8

1. Matthew 23:5.
2. Matthew 6:1–6, 16–18.
3. Romans 8:16; 1 John 3:21.
4. John 19:30.
5. 1 John 2:2.
6. 1 Thessalonians 5:22 KJV.
7. Colossians 2:23, emphasis added.
8. Colossians 2:20–23.
9. Isaiah 29:13.
10. John 14:15.
11. 1 Peter 2:16.
12. Galatians 5:13.
13. 1 Corinthians 8:9, author's rendering.
14. 1 John 4:18.
15. 1 Peter 4:8.

Chapter 9

1. 1 Peter 5:8.
2. Colossians 1:24. Satan didn't stop persecuting Christ just because he ascended to heaven. We are his body, and thus become the lightning rod of Satan's attack.
3. Ephesians 2:1–3.
4. John 17:15–18.
5. 1 Peter 2:11.
6. Colossians 3:1–3.
7. 1 John 2:15–17 NASB.

8. James 4:4.
9. Luke 12:15 KJV.
10. John 8:44; 10:10.
11. James 1:13–15.
12. Romans 12:2.
13. See Isaiah 55:8–9.
14. See 1 Peter 5:8.
15. Ephesians 6:10–18.

Chapter 10

1. Romans 12:2.
2. 1 Corinthians 12:13.
3. 1 John 3:9.
4. Romans 6:3–7.
5. Romans 6:2.
6. James 2:26.
7. 2 Corinthians 5:8.
8. 1 Corinthians 15:51–54; 1 Thessalonians 4:16.
9. 2 Corinthians 5:1–5.
10. 2 Corinthians 5:21.
11. Matthew 13:40; Mark 9:48; Revelation 14:10–11; 20:14–15.
12. 1 Corinthians 15:3; see also Isaiah 53:6.
13. Isaiah 59:2.
14. Hebrews 2:14–15.
15. Romans 6:11. Paul also used this phrase more than twenty times in Ephesians 1 and 2.
16. Galatians 2:20.
17. Romans 8:7–9.
18. Colossians 1:17, emphasis added.

Chapter 11

1. Galatians 2:20.
2. Mark 4:1–20.
3. Ephesians 5:18.
4. See Ephesians 5:19–21.
5. Galatians 5:16 ESV.

6. John 10:10.
7. Psalm 37:4; Matthew 6:33.
8. Galatians 5:25.
9. Ephesians 2:10; Philippians 1:6.

Chapter 12

1. Revelation 22:12.
2. 2 Timothy 3:1–5.
3. Ephesians 4:22.
4. We get the word *rapture* from the Latin translation of the phrase "caught up" in 1 Thessalonians 4:17.
5. Revelation 16:21.
6. 2 Thessalonians 2:11.
7. 2 Thessalonians 2:1–3.
8. 2 Thessalonians 2:3.
9. 2 Thessalonians 2:3 NASB.
10. Revelation 11:7.
11. Daniel 9:26 NASB.
12. 1 John 2:18, 22 NLT.
13. Daniel 11:37.
14. The other was Judas Iscariot. See John 13:27.
15. Matthew 24:36–39.
16. Matthew 24:39.
17. Ezekiel 38–39.
18. Revelation 19:19.
19. Revelation 19:8, 14.
20. Revelation 19:11.
21. Revelation 19:12 NLT.
22. Revelation 19:13.
23. Revelation 14:20; 19:15, 17–18.
24. Revelation 19:16.
25. Revelation 1:7.
26. 1 John 4:7–8.
27. Psalm 2; 78:49; 90:7.
28. John 3:36; Ephesians 2:3.
29. Ephesians 2:4–6.
30. John 12:35.

DISCUSSION GUIDE

Chapter 1

1. Do you agree or disagree that all humans have evil in them? Why?
2. Why do you think some people are more evil than others?
3. What keeps the evil inside us contained?
4. Do you think it's "fair" that we inherited Adam's sin nature and the consequences associated with it? Support your answer.
5. Is it accurate to say that we naturally "hate God"?
6. Had you been Adam or Eve, how might you have responded to the serpent's temptation? What about the second time he tempted you? The twentieth? The two hundredth?
7. What consequences of being a sinner bother you the most?

Chapter 2

1. Where do you see the effects of sin in your family, school, or work?

2. Where do you see it most in your own life? What doesn't "work right"?
3. How does sin personally affect your spirit? Mind? Emotions? Will?
4. What do you think Paul meant when he said, "None seeks for God"?
5. How do you subtly or covertly reject God in your own life?
6. Why do you suppose we don't talk much about sin and being sinners?
7. Why is it not a good idea to compare yourself (your goodness or badness) to others?

Chapter 3

1. After reading Romans 7:15–20, in what sense can you identify with Paul?
2. In what way are we sort of spiritual "schizophrenics"? Why is this so?
3. What frustrates and confuses you about yourself the most?
4. What are your biggest areas of struggle and how does your sin nature mislead you?
5. What happens to the sin nature over time?
6. Why would this struggle cause you to question the reality of your faith?
7. What does this "war" look like in the heart of a believer?
8. In what way is recognizing the reality of this internal war a great first step to winning it?

Chapter 4

1. Why didn't Jesus blame culture for our sins?

2. What does this realization do to change your perspective of sin, self, and society?
3. Does it surprise you to discover that sex was so prevalent in the first century? Why or why not?
4. Why do you think sexuality is such a "narcotic"? Think of as many reasons as you can.
5. Where do you see a relationship between drug use and idolatry/demonology? How does recreational drug use contribute to this?
6. Looking back at Paul's list of "social sins," where do you see the most impact in your particular social network of friends?

Chapter 5

1. In what ways would you say your heart deceives you? Be specific.
2. Would you agree or disagree with the expression "Follow your heart"? Why?
3. Why is the pursuit of absolute freedom not a healthy life choice?
4. In what sense is this pursuit actually a form of slavery?
5. Why can't you fully trust your own heart?
6. What does it promise you but rarely deliver?
7. Can you think of some ways to know your heart better, and thus protect yourself from its deceptions?

Chapter 6

1. Describe your understanding of "authenticity."
2. What troubles you the most about the beast living in your heart pit?

3. What would you be embarrassed for someone to find on the floor there?
4. Why is it so critical to admit the existence of this creature and the fact that he is a part of you?
5. How does doing this help you begin to deal with sin?
6. In what ways does your life revolve around you (in a negative way)?
7. Why don't you need a "radical testimony" in order to be passionate about Christ? What do you need instead?
8. How does an understanding of the depth of your sin motivate you toward great love for Jesus?

Chapter 7

1. Who have been the top three influences in your life so far?
2. What made them so influential? How have they influenced you?
3. In what ways do you find it difficult to "swim upstream" against the current of your culture?
4. How do you imagine things were different for Christians living in the first century? Do you suppose you have it more or less difficult than they did? Explain.
5. Why do you think a person's friends are the most powerful influences in his or her life?
6. Where is your greatest area of weakness when it comes to social influences?
7. Can you identify the attitude that most draws you away from God? How is recognizing this critical to helping you fight it?

Chapter 8

1. What about "religion" bothers you?
2. How did the Jewish leaders corrupt the faith of their fathers? How did Jesus respond to them? How did he describe them?
3. Do you think Christianity has been similarly corrupted in the past? If so, in what ways? What about in your lifetime?
4. In your opinion, how are rules misused in the church today?
5. How can being busy doing God's work actually draw us away from him?
6. Why can't Christian activity change God's view of you and your standing before him?
7. Explain the difference between "obeying the rules" and "being obedient" to God? What motivates each of these?
8. What does God desire before outward obedience? Why?

Chapter 9

1. What about Satan surprises you the most?
2. Of all his names, which one do you feel most applies to the way he usually works against you?
3. What do you think are some of his most effective strategies? How do you see him at work around you: with friends, coworkers, classmates, or family?
4. In what sense are society and culture set up to feed your inner zombie 24/7?
5. Why doesn't God just take us out of the world? Why stay?
6. How do Satan and the world he controls partner with your sin nature's desires? How are you tempted to "conform"?

Chapter 10

1. How would you describe the cause of the inner struggle between sin and righteousness?
2. What are the biggest mistakes (fails) we can make when confronting the subject of the sin nature?
3. Why is trying harder and being more disciplined not the answer?
4. What's the meaning of "Spirit baptism"? What difference does it really make for you—positionally and practically?
5. In what sense are you "dead" to sin and the sin nature? What was Jesus' role in all this?
6. If this is true, then why do you still sin?
7. In what ways is Jesus the answer to your dilemma?

Chapter 11

1. Have you ever known someone to "bail" on Jesus? Why do you think he or she did this? What's the person's explanation? Would you agree with it or would you have your own explanation?
2. What's the real reason we drift away from a relationship with Christ?
3. How would you know if Jesus is a passing "fad" in your life?
4. How would you put in your own words what it means to "let go and walk"? Why is it necessary to do this?
5. How is your identity in Christ linked to these choices?

Chapter 12

1. Do you feel as if you are living in the end times? Why or why not?

2. What about Paul's description of the last days parallels what you see happening in the world around you?

3. What is the significance of Christ's return for his bride as it relates to the church? To the world?

4. What would you say to someone who skeptically thinks Christ will never come back?

5. Why do you suppose God will bring about the judgments listed in the book of Revelation? What's the point?

6. What will happen to your inner zombie when you die or when Jesus returns for you?

7. How has this book given you confidence and hope that you can daily slay your inner zombie?

ABOUT THE AUTHOR

Jeff Kinley began fighting zombies in high school and since then has experienced more than thirty years of active battle. Pastor, speaker (MainThingMinistries.com), author of more than a dozen books, podcast host, and missionary to his midtown neighborhood's "Next Generation Tribe" (VintageNxt. com), Jeff finds every way possible to communicate Christ's grace. Jeff lives in a 1923 cottage with his wife, their three sons, and Mac the Labradoodle.

Jeff is a graduate of the University of Arkansas and Dallas Theological Seminary.

The CHRISTIAN ZOMBIE KILLERS

The Event

The Christian Zombie Killers Weekend
The perfect youth evangelism event

Youth leaders, visit www.ZombieKillersHandbook.com
for more details on how to book Jeff Kinley to be the featured
speaker at your next retreat, camp or D-Now weekend.

The Soundtrack

Indie artists from Dallas to New York have come
together to produce a one-of-a-kind tribute to
The Christian Zombie Killers Handbook.

Visit www.ZombieKillersHandbook.com for more details.